A Singapore Life

A Singapore Life

Harold S. P. Lim

iUniverse, Inc.
New York Lincoln Shanghai

A Singapore Life

Copyright © 2006 by Constance Lim

iUniverse books may be ordered through booksellers or by contacting:

iUniverse
2021 Pine Lake Road, Suite 100
Lincoln, NE 68512
www.iuniverse.com
1-800-Authors (1-800-288-4677)

ISBN-13: 978-0-595-41355-3 (pbk)
ISBN-13: 978-0-595-85705-0 (ebk)
ISBN-10: 0-595-41355-2 (pbk)
ISBN-10: 0-595-85705-1 (ebk)

Printed in the United States of America

To my grandsons,

Deniz & Alex Lim-Sersan

Contents

Editor's Foreword

THIS book began with a request for bedtime stories for my two young sons. My father began e-mailing them stories weekly, describing events from his childhood that he thought would interest them. As his audience quickly grew, though, he soon moved from telling children's tales to relating the story of his life. All in all, he sent some 130 episodes over three years. This book is a compilation of the episodes covering his earlier years, from childhood to his first attempts to make a life for himself in post-war Singapore.

In reading my father's story, I was struck by the difference between the Singapore he described and the Singapore that we see today. Singapore today is a "developed" city-state with one of Asia's highest standards of living. When you wander through the housing estates or the business district of today's built-up Singapore, it is hard to believe that the island was once mostly jungle and swamp, and that people made a living off the land.

This book stands as one small record of the former natural environment of Singapore, and how it affected the lives of people in the past. This book also provides a glimpse of life on the island in the first half of the twentieth century, a quarter century before the establishment of an independent state with its own national identity. Although Singapore has changed greatly since, culturally, socially, and politically, this period and the generation that grew of age then played an important part in the making of today's Singapore.

Since this is a memoir, I have mostly retained the terminology, spellings (especially of Malay words and place names), and the slightly idiosyncratic transcriptions of the Chinese Hokkien dialect common during the period. As much as possible, I have left Singaporean idioms and vocabulary in the text, only editing occasionally to make the book more accessible to readers in other countries.

Some readers of the book in manuscript form expressed concern about the book's descriptions of the treatment of certain animals. It should be noted that this book merely relates events that once took place, from the perspective of the observer at that time, and does not in any way advocate such treatment of animals.

Thanks are due to many friends and family for their encouragement and support. In particular, P. Whimster in Ottawa, V. Foo in New York, and A. Wong in Vancouver gave generously of their time and expertise.

Constance Lim
Ottawa, Canada, 2006

Preface

Tell me not, in mournful numbers,
Life is but an empty dream!—

. . . .

Life is real! Life is earnest!

Henry Wadsworth Longfellow, "A Psalm of Life"

NOW in my eighties and living in Canada, the events of my early life, so real and earnest then, are far away in time and place.

But memories of those early years in Singapore still surprise me by their strength. Some vivid, some faint, they emerge, one after another, as if to remind me of their share in my life, and to assert their place in the world.

And so, I have set them down in paper here, those moments of sweet innocence, the joys and sadness of growing up, the successes and failures I met in the path I took. Here is the story of my Singapore life.

It is my hope that as others read this book, they will remember similar situations that they met, and recall even more of their lives and how their experiences shaped them.

This book would not have been possible without the efforts of my daughter, Constance Lim, and her two children, Deniz and Alex, in Ottawa. Thanks are also due to the many others who gave their encouragement and support: my sons, Roland and David; my niece, Jean Chan, and her husband, Archie, in Canberra, Australia; and my nephew, Joshua Lim, and his wife, Maud, in Singapore; other relatives; and many friends, especially (Raju) Narayana Narayana and Lee Kip Lee.

Any mistakes in this book are due to my poor memory. Please rest assured that the memories are faithful to the spirit of the event, if not always in the details.

Harold S. P. Lim
Vancouver, B.C., Canada, 2006

A Singapore Life

First Years

M Y boyhood days were the happiest in my life. Without a care in the world, I roamed everywhere, barefoot, and clad in singlet and shorts. Being the youngest son, I was the favourite, and was well pampered by my older sisters and brothers (nine of them). My whole world was composed of boyish delights: playing hide-and-seek, shooting marbles, flying kites, and spinning tops. When I was older, there were days of sadness as my sisters left home for Seremban to continue their studies. But there was not a single worry or responsibility on my head, and the days passed so quickly.

At first, we lived in a big bungalow on a fruit plantation at the end of Kim Chuan Avenue. There were many durian, mango, and mangosteen trees around the house, and the plantation was next to a sheep farm. We had lots of fun playing hide-and-seek in the rambling grounds.

To start, we stood in a circle, hands behind our backs. After a ritual chant, we showed our hands, either palms up or down. Those with the same side up (or down, if we chose) were out and became the "hiders." We repeated this ritual until one person remained: this was the "seeker."

The seeker would *buang gayong*;[1] that is, throw a milk or cigarette tin partly filled with stones, as far away as possible. While he or she went to retrieve the tin, the others ran to hide. After returning the tin to the starting point, the seeker would search for the hiders, rushing back to shake the tin on finding one. The hiders would try to sneak back and shake the tin without the seeker noticing. On hearing the tin rattling, everyone would know the game was over. With so many nooks and corners in and around the house, there were plenty of places to hide.

Sometimes, while playing, we would hear a sound—*boop*. Everyone would abandon the game and run to find the durian or mango that had fallen. There would be squeals of laughter and delight, and whoever found it would shout with triumph and joy. You can imagine the noise made by five or six children in their pursuit of the fallen fruit. When all the noise and excitement had quietened down, the fruit was shared among all the players, but the finder had the biggest share of all, and he or she was the hero of the day.

---

[1] Editor's note: Malay, *buang* "throw," *gayong* "tin."

When I was about five, my mother wanted to visit her homeland and show her aged parents their grandson (me). As we were about to board the ship to China, my sister Soon Geok wanted to go, too. She cried and cried, and in the end, my mother had to take her along, and she had to miss her schooling.

We met with heavy seas on the journey. Everyone seemed to be seasick, but I was well and running about. Nearing Hong Kong, our ship was caught in a typhoon. For days and nights, the ship was heaving and swaying, and almost swallowed by the waves. Cargo was dumped into the sea, and the passengers thought the end was near. When all seemed lost, the typhoon suddenly abated, and we reached Hong Kong safely. The ship, the *Hong Hoa,* sank in a typhoon on a later journey.

We travelled by rail, in a pumpcar (a railway car propelled by a man pumping on a lever) to my parents' native town, Chiangchiu, Hokkien.[2] My mother's family was reasonably well off. The family home was a brick house surrounded by an orchard of fruit trees (mostly lychee and longan). My grandmother used to sit at the doorstep of her house, and every morning, I would dutifully greet her and wish her "Good morning." She would give me a few pennies, which I usually spent buying sweets when the hawker came round. My uncles would carry me on their shoulders when they went to exercise in gyms or in the parks.

The longan trees were huge and full of fruit, which we plucked and put into sacks. We kept a sack in the house, and I gorged on longans for days. The house had two wells, one with cold water, and the other, warm. The family put lychees and longans in the "cold" well overnight. When we took the fruit out in the morning, they were chilled and delicious. Water from the "warm" well was used for cooking.

One day, there was a flood, and we had to stay on the second floor for days. The ground floor was covered with water. It was fortunate that we had a brick house. It did not crumble as many other houses did. Otherwise, I might not have been able to write this story.

I do not know about my father's family as I did not meet his relatives, but they must also have been of reasonable means of living, or he would not have been able to marry my mother. Still, I wonder why and how my father made the move to Singapore.

In the late 1800s, my father, Lim Teck Boo, left southern China with his wife to settle in Singapore, then part of the Straits Settlements, a British crown colony. Adventurous and brave spirits they were, to leave their comfortable homes to start a new life in a strange land with different languages

---

[2] Editor's note: The place names are transliterated from the Chinese Min-nan dialect commonly known as Hokkien. Chiangchiu is Zhangzhou City in Fujian Province.

and customs, where they had no other relatives. They often told us children that they arrived in Singapore with nothing except a bundle of clothing.

One by one, we children were born in Singapore, and our family roots were established in the new land. But where did my father find the resources to buy his first house on Kim Chuan Avenue, with its mango and durian trees, and even a horse-drawn carriage in those early days? How he managed to feed, educate and bring up all his children is still a mystery to me.

There were six sons and four daughters in the family. I was the last child, born in 1924. Not long after, the slump of the 1930s was felt all over the country. To all general appearances, we were well-to-do; Father by then had built a fine house on a coconut estate and at one time owned rubber and pineapple estates at Lim Chu Kang. But we had no money to spare. There were heavy mortgages to pay, and many mouths to feed. I was told later that my father lost his rubber and pineapple estates in the 1930s.

A rich "uncle" (he could have been a relative or just a family friend) who lived in Medan, Indonesia, visited us yearly. My uncle and aunt liked me very much and would bring me to their cruise ship and give me many presents whenever they visited. When I was older, my mother and sister told me often that my uncle and aunt had offered to "adopt" me as their child—that is, they had proposed to buy me for a sum of money. But my mother refused their offer, although the money would have been useful to feed so many children. Once, Uncle and Aunt gave me a gold pocket watch, but my mother took it away and returned it to them, saying I was too small to keep such a valuable present.

Home

The Estate

AFTER living for some time in the bungalow on Kim Chuan Avenue, my father built a new house on an estate nearby. The estate had forty acres of land, through which ran a road and a stream between two hills. Our house was built on one of the hills. Father kept about an acre around it for his garden. The other thirty-nine acres were planted with rubber trees when we first moved in, but these were later replaced with coconut trees.

A path from the back of our house led down to the road—an uneven mud track with many potholes—that ran through the estate. Along the road were houses belonging to other families, some on Father's estate, and some, further down, on other private land. Those families with houses on Father's estate paid him rent for the use of the land (although their houses were their own). Across the road from our house was a shop belonging to one Ah Chan, from whom we usually bought our groceries.

This new house was Father's dream house, and he planned his garden to be his "Garden of Eden." There was a big gate at the entrance, and in the garden, he planted his favourite fruit trees: rambutan, banana, cherry, soursop, and guava. He also planted *berlimbing* (starfruit) trees around the badminton court at the back of the house, and a clump of sugar cane along the edge of the banana trees. Across the footpath leading down the hill, he planted three *jambu ayer* (rose apple trees), and near the vegetable garden, a *jambu wangi* (a more fragrant variety of the rose apple). Along the road leading to our house, he planted a row of dwarf coconut trees that bore small, yellow coconuts.

The house actually consisted of two buildings with a small courtyard in between. A flight of stone steps led up to the entrance of the house in the larger building. At the front was a circular sitting room with twelve windows. A wide corridor with two bedrooms along each side linked this circular sitting room to another sitting room at the back of the house. One bedroom led to a study, and another to a small "secret room" with a trap door concealing a spiral staircase to the ground floor. Attached to the smaller sitting room at the back was yet another bedroom. A cement staircase led down from the sitting room at the back to the smaller, second building of the house, which held the kitchen, a dining room, a bathroom, and a storeroom, all on the ground floor.

A covered area close to this second building served as the toilet area. In the early days, the toilet waste was deposited in buckets, and a man would come regularly to collect the full buckets and replace them with empty ones. Later, the toilet area was moved, when my father had a deep hole drilled in the ground a small distance away from the house, and an outhouse built around the hole.

The ground floor of the larger building was divided into two sections. The larger section, about two thirds of the area, had a ceiling of just four feet, and was used for storage. Going into this section, I often bumped my head against the beams when I forgot to bend down.

The other section was at a slightly lower level, a few steps down. Here, Father kept a rubber mangle and trays for curing raw rubber. In the days when the estate was a rubber plantation, hired men and women would go out early in the morning to tap the rubber trees. When they returned, they poured the liquid rubber that they had collected into the trays, adding acid to make the rubber coagulate. When the rubber solidified, the flat pieces were pressed through the mangle to produce sheets of different thicknesses (there were screws to adjust the space between the rollers of the mangle). The sheets were then hung to dry on wires strung beneath the ceiling.

Our house, like most houses then, did not have glass windows. Whenever it rained, my job as a boy was to close the wooden window shutters of the house. "Ah Poh, the windows![3] Quickly!" my mother would call when the rain started. Even if she did not call, I would rush to the job. With so many rooms in the house, it took a while to go from room to room to pull the shutters together carefully, without banging, and to secure them one by one. By the time I finished, the wooden floor in some rooms would be wet from the rain beating in, and I had to mop the water up.

There was no electricity in the house, and we used kerosene lamps for light. I was proud when I was chosen to pump the pressure lamps. We slept under mosquito nets, as there were plenty of mosquitoes flying in the night. We had, of course, at that time, never seen or heard of TV, and had no radio. Our water did not come from taps; instead, we had to draw water from a well two to three hundred feet down the hill.

The well had a three-foot wall built around it to prevent people from falling in. The water was thirty or so feet deep in the ground. We drew water using a

---

[3] She was calling me by my personal name, "Poh." In Chinese, it is common to add the prefix "Ah" to a personal name. See footnote 9 for more on Chinese names.

bucket tied to a rope that was anchored to the ground. Leaning over the wall, we would lower the bucket into the well. When the bucket reached the water, we would let loose enough rope for the bucket to lie on its side. Then, with a swift flick of the hand, we would pull the rope in such a way that the bucket flipped over so that water could flow into it. It was quite an art.

We then had to pull the rope up slowly, one hand after the other, until the bucket, full of water, reached the rim of the wall. We would lean over to grip the handle of the bucket, and, with a final heave, bring the full bucket over the three-foot wall. Sometimes, if we were not careful or misjudged the clearance, the bottom of the bucket would catch the wall, and the water would spill as the bucket tipped. Then we would have to start all over again.

When the bucket cleared the wall, we poured the water into a four-gallon kerosene tin. We carried the tin up the hill to the house, where we poured the water into a very large earthenware jar with a wooden cover. It was hard work carrying the water the few hundred feet up to the house. Water then was very precious to us, and we used it carefully and sparingly.

As a small boy, I often helped my mother throw the bucket into the well. When it was full of water, I tried to pull it up, but did not have enough strength. I was able to do it when I grew bigger. However, I had to work at tipping the bucket in the well. Daily, I tried it again and again to perfect my skill. When I mastered the technique, I was as happy as if I had won the lottery.

Later, when Father finally installed a pump with pipes leading to the house, life was a little bit easier, but we still had to turn a wheel to pump up the water.

When there was a drought, neighbours all around us came to help themselves from our well. Filling water in kerosene tins and carrying them away on bamboo poles, they drew water until there was no more. However, the well would fill up again during the night, and the next morning it would be full again. The well never ran dry.

There were two ponds on the estate, each the size of a tennis court. On the slope above one of the ponds, Father built pigsties, where he kept pigs. The pigs thrived on our leftovers and often feasted on the trunks of banana trees. Father's banana trees around the house provided our family with delicious bananas, but the trees were chopped down once they no longer bore fruit. The leaves were sold to Indians for use as mats and plates in their restaurants, while the soft and pulpy banana trunk was chopped into small pieces and boiled in a huge cauldron outdoors, close to the pigsties.

Father would light firewood under the cauldron, put in the pieces of chopped banana trunk, and add bran (*k'ng*) or dried coconut waste (*iah p'o*).[4] This *iah p'o* came in round slabs about two inches thick and three feet in diameter. Father stirred the concoction in the cauldron with a long, oar-like piece of wood.

In the pond by the pigsties, he grew water hyacinth, floating plants with beautiful blue flowers. The plants grew rapidly and in no time covered most of the pond. He used the plants as food for the pigs. As the plants were rich in proteins and vitamins, the pigs thrived on them. When the pigs were given a bath, the pigsties were washed as well, and the water would flow down to the pond, in turn providing nutrients for the plants.

My father reared carp in the ponds as well. There were about six to eight carp ponds along the road that ran through our estate, and from the pond-owners (our neighbours), Father bought carp fry to stock his ponds. He harvested the carp once a year, just before the Chinese New Year, when he could sell them at a good price. Some of the carp harvest he returned to the pond to keep as stock, and some we would take home for ourselves to eat. The rest, he sold. He also sold pigs just before the festive season.

Hired men came once a year to help. They gathered the hyacinth plants and also fed and bathed the pigs. Most of the gathered plants were chopped into small pieces, to be fed to the pigs, but some were set aside in a tank, to be thrown back to the pond later as stock. Once the hyacinth plants had been collected from the pond, two men would wade into the water, pulling between them a long net spanning the width of the pond. The net had floats along the top edge and weights along the bottom. The men stretched the net across the water, letting the weighted edge sink to the bottom of the pond. Then, they dragged the net from one end of the pond to the other. Some fish managed to escape by jumping over the net as it was being dragged across the pond, but most were corralled to the end of the pond, where they were easily caught by hand.

To gather what fish remained in the water, the men would drain the pond. They dug a channel, about one foot wide and two feet deep, beginning at a nearby stream and working towards the pond. Just before they reached the pond, they stopped digging and placed a sluice gate and a net across the end of the incomplete channel. Then, they continued digging to link the channel to the pond.

With the channel complete, once they lifted the gate, the water from the pond would immediately rush through the channel and drain into the stream. The remaining fish would be trapped in the pond by the net across the chan-

---

[4] Editor's note: Hokkien words.

nel. When most of the water had drained out, and the fish could be seen swimming and struggling in the shallow water remaining in the pond, the men closed the sluice gate and collected the fish.

When the water in the pond was nearly all gone, I would wade in and was sometimes almost up to my waist in mud, trying to catch some fish for myself. I managed to catch some *chikak* (a flat flounder-like fish, about three to four times larger than an angel fish), *lei hee* (a beautiful, strong fish about eight to twelve inches long, shaped like a cucumber) and catfish (*torsat,* "mudfish," in Hokkien, or *ikan sembilan* in Malay).

The catfish were difficult to catch with bare hands. You needed some skill to avoid being pierced by their poisonous fins, which were about an inch long and very sharp. You had to get hold of the fish by placing your thumb in front of the head and one finger on each side of the fish behind the fins. If you just grabbed at the fish, the two fins would stab into your hand, and it would hurt.

After catching some fish, which I put in a bottle-necked rattan basket hung at my side, I would rush home and give them to my mother. She would scale the fish (except for the catfish, as they have no scales) and prepare them for a meal.

We would feast on fish, rice, soup, and vegetables from my father's vegetable garden for many days.

Not to be outdone, my mother reared chickens and ducks at the back of the house. We had a henhouse in a shed near the house. The shed had parallel bars on which the roosters and hens would roost for the night. The hens would sit in the many baskets and lay their eggs, cackling away to announce the fact. When we children heard the cackling, we knew that there were fresh eggs, and would often run to collect them for Mother. Sometimes, if Mother was not around and we had already collected many eggs, I would crack a small hole at one end of an egg and suck out the warm egg white and yolk inside. It was really very delicious.

One night, when we needed eggs for supper, Mother went to the henhouse and felt under the sitting hens for eggs. As we had no electricity, she was groping in the dark. Suddenly she felt something cold. She rushed back to the house and returned with a lantern to discover a python coiled up in place of the hen. She called for help, and my father and brothers came. They caught the python and put it in a sack.

The next morning, one of my "uncles" (a family friend) came and strung the snake up on a pole. We gazed in wonder at the ten-foot long creature. Uncle cut up the snake and cooked it with some herbs. We had snake soup for a couple of days. It tasted better than chicken soup, and we thought it was because the snake had eaten the hen.

Family

I remember my mother as a kind and good mother, but very strict. If we did any wrong, she did not spare her cane. I felt the sting of her cane more than once when I was late coming back for dinner.

She took good care of all ten of us children without a grumble or complaint. She cooked our meals, sewed our clothes, and washed our clothes at the well near our house. She even ironed them with a hot iron containing burning coals. She went marketing on foot, fed the chickens, and collected the eggs. She saw to our every need. She instilled in us a sense of responsibility and hard work, and brought us up with a sense of fairness to all. We all respected and loved her.

A staunch Christian, she attended the Paya Lebar Methodist Church every Sunday. She sang hymns in Hokkien, using both the Chinese and romanized Hokkien versions[5] of the hymnbook. She was always reading the Bible and encouraged me to do so also. Dressed in Chinese *samfu*,[6] a white top, fastened at one side with cloth buttons, and black trousers, she went out visiting the parish, often on foot, together with other "Bible women."[7]

One Sunday, she was invited to preach in church. I saw her poring over and marking her Bible in preparation. I wondered how she would do it. I need not have feared for her. On that day, with a clear voice, she preached a sermon and quoted many verses from the Bible in support of her message. Everyone including myself was much impressed.

Mother organized prayer meetings in the circular hall at our house and at Ng Phek Hioh's *mee-hoon* (rice vermicelli) factory on Kim Chuan Avenue. We had an old piano in our hall and a manual organ that we sometimes used. My mother would invite visiting pastors and the "Bible women" to our house.

One of these Bible women was Tan Phek Giok, recently arrived from China. This young woman preacher nearly died in a fire when she was a child. Her face was badly burnt and disfigured, but she recovered, became a Christian, and committed her life to preaching and saving people's souls. Mother heard about her and invited her to stay at our house. Popularly known as Miss Tan, she was the first woman to be ordained (later) as a minister in the Methodist Church in Singapore. As a boy, I was often called to ferry her on my bicycle to

---

[5] Versions in which Hokkien words were transliterated in the Roman alphabet.

[6] A Chinese woman's suit

[7] These were women serving in the ministry. In those days, women could not be ordained as ministers.

the Ongs' house, about a mile away, along a winding footpath, over a hill and through a little valley. The road was narrow and pitted with holes. It was tricky to cycle and balance with her sitting on the bar in front of me. When we reached the hill, just by a jackfruit tree, I had to get down and push the bicycle up the slope with her still on the bar. It was hard work as I was only a boy not yet in my teens. It was worth it when she praised me and told everyone what I had done.

Being the youngest child, I was my mother's favourite. She took me with her to church every Sunday. I learned from her to sing hymns and to read the Bible in romanized Hokkien. I was also her errand boy. Whenever she needed something from the shop, or to pass messages or gifts to friends, she would call for me and send me on the task. I was always keen to do her bidding.

Mother was a good cook. No one complained about her food. She often cooked a big pot of *tau iu ba'* (pork in soya sauce), which was delicious and more so if some *tau foo* (tofu) were added. Vegetables were simple and mostly *ing chye* (water cress) with *hay bee* (dried shrimp). Sometimes we had long beans and *ba' tau* (flat beans), or *brinjal* (eggplant) from Father's vegetable garden. Occasionally, we had chicken and eggs from mother's chicken coop.

It was simple food, and the dishes were left on the table, covered with a domed net to keep away the flies. Even when the food was cold, it tasted delicious, as I was always hungry.

We had no fridge or microwave then, and I had to boil all our drinking water. This meant building a fire (from charcoal), doling water with a scoop into the kettle from the big jar where we kept water drawn from the well, and boiling the water over the burning coal. We had a few vacuum flasks on the table for keeping hot water. Tea was in a Chinese teapot, in a pretty tea-cozy to keep it warm.

The "*tic toc*" man sometimes came around the neighbourhood. We would hear him in the distance, knocking on a piece of bamboo, going "*tic toc, tic toc, tic toc…*" Once, my sister told me to call him over. He came, pedalling a three-wheel cycle, pulling his elaborate stall holding pots, pans, foodstuff, and a charcoal stove. I was curious, and found out that he was a friendly fellow.

My sister ordered a bowl of noodles. He put some *mee* (noodles), bean sprouts, and dried prawns into a large meshed ladle and placed the ladle into a boiling pot for some minutes. Then he took the ladle out and emptied its contents in a bowl. He added some soup from another pot, a little pepper and some spice, and gave it to my sister. My sister let me have some of the noodles and, oh my, I was in heaven. It was so delicious. It was the first time I tasted hawker food.

Daily, I ate three big bowls of rice and *tau iu ba'* with relish. I was not a "difficult eater." I remember my first sister-in-law (that is, my eldest brother's wife) and my sister Bian feeding me my meals in the garden when I was about three years old. After one spoonful, I would run about the flowers, and they would follow, chasing after me with the bowl of food to give me the next spoonful. Whenever they caught up with me, I ate without complaint, and they were happy and pleased with me. What a good boy I was.

My Father was known as a teacher and preacher, but as far as I know, he never taught at any school, and the one and only time I heard him preach was at the Presbyterian Church on Kim Chuan Road.[8] Together with Ng Kim Chuan (after whom both Kim Chuan Road and Kim Chuan Avenue were named), he was an elder of the church. He walked the three miles to church from our house every Sunday.

Dressed simply, in a white, drill Chinese coat with cotton buttons and long trousers, he did not appear or behave as a rich man, although at one time he had pineapple and rubber estates at Lim Chu Kang. He never had much money to spare; all his money was invested in his land, and his advice to me in later years was, "Buy land."

He rolled his own tobacco cigarettes. Most evenings, he would walk the mile and a half to his favourite jaunt, a wine shop on Paya Lebar Road. There he would spend an hour or two, enjoying his wine with peanuts, before walking back home. He carried a hardwood walking stick (an "iron stick," he called it), which he said was for protection against dogs and other dangers.

Some evenings, he stayed home, reading newspapers and drinking his Hennessy brandy. He could finish half a bottle neat without any trouble. We children would gather around him, and he would ask me, especially, to pound his back, after which he would give me a few coppers (I think he wanted to give me money but had to find an excuse to do so). After his drink, he would go to sleep, and very soon, his snores could be heard all over the house.

---

[8] The church my father attended was "liberal" and allowed drinking and smoking. Mother may have branched off to a Methodist Church as she had more friends in it.

The ten of us sons and daughters in the family were each spaced about two years apart. The eldest, my brother Siew Guan, was about twenty years older than me, the youngest child.

One by one, my elder brothers and sisters established their independent lives as I grew into childhood. Siew Guan became a dresser (a doctor's assistant) in the hospital, Soon Teck a nurse in Seremban (in Malaya), and Siew Hui chief clerk in the Police Department. Soon Bian took up nursing at Muar, Siew Ek became a lab assistant in the Municipal Building, Soon Suat took up studies at Raffles College, Siew Tee and Siew Boon became school teachers, and Soon Geok went to study at the Malayan Seminary.[9]

My eldest brother, Siew Guan, bought a radio and invited us to his house in government quarters on Outram Road to listen to it. I was very excited, as at the old house, there was no electricity and no radio. I was fascinated to hear music and voices coming from a magic cabinet bearing the letters HMV, a dial, and two, three turning knobs. It was so wonderful and amazing to me that I stayed up late into the night listening to it.

My eldest sister, Soon Teck, visited us once a year after she moved to Seremban. The first time she came, she gave me a colourful money box made out of a coconut shell. The shell was full of shillings. I had never seen, let alone been given, so many coins in my life. I was overjoyed and felt very rich. Now and then during the fruit season, Eldest Sister[10] would send us, through the railway, a big rattan basket full of durians, rambutans and mangosteens. I would go with my brothers to the Tanjong Pagar railway station to collect the basket. We really enjoyed the fruit.

One day, Father was all excited and seemed very pleased with himself. When we asked him what the good news was, he told us to wait and see. We waited month after month, but there was no news, and Father seemed a bit anxious and less happy.

---

[9] According to Chinese custom, the family name comes first, then the generational name (each child in the family has a name common to that generation), then the personal name. In my generation, *Siew* was used for the boys and *Soon* for the girls. My full name was *Lim Siew Poh*, *Lim* being my family name, *Siew* my generational name, and *Poh* my personal name.

[10] It is Chinese custom to address siblings by their position in the family.

However, the news came at last. He announced that the road leading to our house was to be named after him. The road would be called "Lim Teck Boo Road." The government had even included our family name, Lim, in the street address, and that made him very proud. He and Ng Kim Chuan had both been pioneers in Paya Lebar, and Kim Chuan had long had his name on the two roads leading to his estate (Kim Chuan Road and Kim Chuan Avenue). Now Father could boast that the road leading to our estate bore his full name; there was *Lim* Teck Boo Road, as compared to plain Kim Chuan Road, without the *Ng*. But Kim Chuan Road was much longer than his! So both of them had one over the other.

Coconuts

COCONUTS, coconuts, the wonder tree of the tropics. The coconut tree is the most valuable palm tree in the tropics. It is the "tree of a thousand uses" (*pokok seribu guna* in Malay)—every part of it can be used.

Young coconuts are green or yellow in colour and weigh about three to five pounds each. Rich in vitamins and enzymes, the water and the flesh of the young coconut can be drunk and eaten fresh. When the nuts turn old, they become grey in colour and are much lighter. Old coconuts can float for miles in water or in the sea. The flesh of the old coconut is dried and called copra. It is used for making soap and cooking oil. Export of copra is one of the main trades of the tropics.

The coconut's leathery trunk and leaves are used for building materials, and its flowers tapped to make toddy, an alcoholic drink. Even the shell of old coconuts can be made into ornaments and trinkets of all kinds, the most popular of which are money boxes for children.

My father's estate was originally planted with rubber trees. As the rubber trees grew old (they have a lifespan of about twenty years), and when the price of rubber fell due to increasing use of synthetic rubber, Father had the foresight to cut them down to sell as firewood. He planted coconut trees to replace them, and after a few years, there were many coconut trees on the estate. He kept on planting more. I think he knew he could depend on coconuts as the mainstay of his income.

Every forty odd days, we harvested the coconuts. If not, the old coconuts would fall by themselves and perhaps damage houses below the trees, or even kill a passer-by. Besides, we lost revenue as well, as whoever came across a coconut would just pick it up and keep it (finders, keepers).

To pluck the coconuts, Ahmad the *kebun* (gardener) would come up from his long, narrow attap house[11] where he lived with his two wives and many children. He tied with rattan several pieces of bamboo into one long pole. This pole was sometimes as long as fifty feet, and had a curved hook tied to its end. Balancing the pole like a circus acrobat, Ahmad would go from one coconut tree to another, and with the hook, shake the bunch of coconuts at the top of the tree. When coconuts are old or ripe, they are ready to drop, and when Ahmad shook the bunch, one or two old coconuts would usually fall. As he was under the tree, he would move to avoid being hit.

---

[11] A type of traditional wooden house with a roof made from leaves of the attap palm.

However, one day, a number of coconuts fell at the same time, and he could not avoid them all. One of them landed on his head, and he was knocked out. It was as if a large wooden ball had dropped from forty feet onto his head. He was not well for many days.

Sometimes one of Ahmad's sons came to help. The son would climb the smaller coconut trees to pluck the nuts and throw them to the ground. He used a belt—a rope about three feet long tied into a loop. After climbing a few feet up a tree, he would place the looped rope across the trunk and slip his feet into the loop, one foot into each end. With the rope tight across the trunk of the tree, he would inch one foot higher, step steady in the belt, then follow with the other foot. Ahmad's son often used this method for climbing after rain, when the coconut trunks were wet and slippery. Sometimes, he also cut steps in the trunk of the coconut trees. Some of the coconut trees were forty to fifty feet high, and would sway in the wind. It was hard work and dangerous.

Once, one of Ahmad's friends brought a monkey tied to a long rope. The monkey climbed up the coconut tree fearlessly, easily, and fast, and began throwing down old coconuts from the tree. It had been trained to twist and throw down just the old coconuts. We were so fascinated watching the monkey that we forgot to look out for the falling coconuts. There were a few close calls! After doing its work, the monkey would get a reward of a banana or two. I thought this was a wonderful way of harvesting coconuts, but Ahmad said he preferred his long bamboo pole, as he would not know how to feed and control the monkey.

A man would carry the harvested coconuts to the compound of our house, using two large rattan baskets, one suspended from each end of a long pole carried over his shoulder. Soon we would have hundreds of coconuts in a big pile in our garden. My father would start selling them, at 8–10c each. Householders and shopkeepers usually knew when we were reaping the coconuts, and they came to buy them at our house. Any coconuts that were not sold then would have their husks stripped.

A man came with a big spear to do the job. He stuck the butt end of the spear firmly into the ground, with the sharp spearhead pointing up, two to three feet above the ground. He picked a coconut and impaled it on the spear. Bracing his thigh (covered by a thick apron) against the speared coconut, he tore a piece of the husk away. He did this again and again until the entire husk was removed. The man would not work when the coconuts were wet, as they became slippery then. If his hands slipped on the coconut while he was tearing the husk away, he could easily cut himself on the spear.

As ordinary householders had difficulty removing the husk themselves, the stripped coconuts were in greater demand. But they cost a little more at 15c each. The husks were sold for various uses, as firewood, as a base for planting orchids, for matting, upholstery, and for making ropes.

To make ropes, the husks were soaked overnight in a large tub. In the morning, the rope-makers (our neighbours, who had a rope-making business) would pound the husks with a stone to separate the fibres from the thick skin. They intertwined the raw fibres into ropes, and stretched the long finished ropes on poles, like telephone lines set low to the ground, to dry in the sun.

During the war years, I tried my hand at making ropes. The fibrous husks were in great demand then, as everyone wanted them for making ropes. I thought it might be an interesting way to make some money for myself. I pounded the husks until my back ached, and my fingers were numbed, stained, and wrinkled. After so much backbreaking work, I was only able to produce one coil of rope. I was reluctant to make more as it was not my cup of tea. I don't know how strong my rope was, but I sold it together with the other ropes made on our estate. At least I had tried it and had produced a rope.

At the side of our house, we had a row of dwarf coconut trees with yellow coconuts. We loved to pluck the young coconuts off one tree in particular, which had the most fragrant fruit. We would slice off the tops of the coconuts with a *parang* (Malay for machete)—young coconuts are easy to cut as their husks are still tender and have not turned fibrous. Then, we would pierce the shell and drink the coconut water straight from the shell. Again using the *parang*, we would then split the coconut into halves and, with a spoon, scrape out the flesh to eat. The flesh was soft, cool, and fragrant, and tasted better than any pudding or jelly I have had.

On a hot day, I used to climb up the tree (it was only about ten feet high), and choose a young, good-sized coconut for myself. How happy and contented I was then, enjoying the fragrant coconut water and the delicious coconut flesh. I felt like a king.

At one time, there was a coconut tree on the estate that needed to be felled. The tree was leaning like the tower of Pisa and was in danger of falling down and crushing the attap house close by. Ahmad the *kebun* tied a rope around the trunk of the tree. Several men stood ready to pull this rope so that the tree, when felled, would fall away from the house. With a long-handled axe, Ahmad cut a groove to direct the fall of the coconut tree. He then made the final swings. With a crash, the tree came tumbling down. But the house was safe.

The Malays took the branches, of which there were about twenty to thirty. They sheared the leaves off the branches, and made brooms out of the ribs of the leaves. The kept the leaves to wrap Malay rice cakes (*ketupat*). Our gardener took a portion of the trunk and laid it across a stream as a bridge. He stacked the remaining pieces to make an embankment around the hill of our house. We cooked part of the tender head of the tree in a delicious curry. We had many young coconuts from the cut tree and enjoyed the refreshing meat for several days.

Nothing of the coconut tree was wasted. No wonder it is known as the tree of life in the tropics.

Early Adventures

Fun and Games

AS the favourite son, I roamed the estate like a boy king, entertaining myself and my friends.

Our pleasures were simple, but gave us endless delight. Sometimes we searched for rubber seeds around the estate. Once we found some, we would rub the seeds on a rough surface and then look for a victim to touch with the heated seed, squealing with laughter at his or her reaction. At times, we would pierce two holes in a seed, through which we threaded two strings. Holding both strings at each end, we would swing the seed around, our hands moving closer together as the strings wound up. Then, moving our hands apart, we would set the seed spinning as the strings unwound. The spinning produced a delightful sound. We made the seed spin one way, then the other, by moving our hands apart and bringing them closer together. It was mesmerizing.

I loved to play marbles. We made three holes in a straight line in the ground, each a few feet apart. Then, from a distance, facing the holes in a straight line, we tried to sink our marbles into the holes, knocking aside opponents' marbles that were in the way. We played a nine-hole game, progressing from the first hole, to the second, and then the third, three times round. I practiced for days and won so many marbles that I had quite a pile of them—my first treasures in life.

I was also a champion at *chatek*. A *chatek* is a toy made out of two or three chicken feathers squeezed tight, at the end of their quills, through the middle of a one-inch thick pile of small paper discs. The idea behind the game was to kick the *chatek* and try to keep it in the air as long as possible.[12] You could also do fancy moves, kicking the *chatek* with different parts of the foot or leg, spinning around between kicks, or whatever else you could think of. Once I kicked the *chatek* more than 100 times, keeping it in the air all this time without it touching the ground.

---

[12] Similar to the game of hackeysack.

For rounders, we stuck three sticks in the ground to form a large triangle, and spread players (fielders) all around the field. The thrower would throw the ball gently to the batter, who stood a small distance away from the first stick. Once the batter hit the ball, he tried to run to touch each stick and then back to his starting point as fast as he could. The fielders would try to hit the batter with the ball as he was running. We used an old tennis ball and a wooden stick. I found it great fun either hitting the ball as the batter, or catching the ball as a fielder.

One day my brothers gave me a football. We played barefoot, with two stones to mark the goalposts. I kicked the ball with the side of my foot. Often I would miss and stump my right toe. Ouch, it hurt—but it was soon forgotten, and we were off chasing the ball.

I met two friends while playing football in the field near Kim Chuan Avenue. They were Yuen Poh and Kheng Seng, and they lived on Kim Chuan Avenue. They came to the house often, and we had good times playing together. I would call on them and visit their homes, too. My parents knew Kheng Seng's grandfather, Reverend Tay, well through church. Kheng Seng was an only son, while Yuen Poh came from a rich family. Compared to me, they were both sheltered and unused to country life. I became their leader, as I knew all the different boys' games. I could also make birdcalls and whistle tunes with a constant tremolo, which they tried to copy but could never succeed. When they came over, I would take them to climb the *jambu wangi* tree, and we would sit on its branches, talking about my marbles, tops, catapults, kites, birds, fish, and so forth.

I also made friends with the children of Ahmad the *kebun*, who lived down the road leading past our house, about 200 yards away. One of his sons, Hassan, was slightly older than me, but we became good friends. He taught me much about the fish, birds, and plants around the estate. When I couldn't find any boys to play with, I sometimes played hopscotch with my sister Geok, and with Hassan's sisters, who would come up to our house to pluck cherries from our tree.

I found other playmates among the children of the many families living along the road leading past our house to Paya Lebar Road. When Father bought his first car (for the princely sum of some nine hundred dollars), these children used to climb on the running board of the car to hitch a free ride. It became a nuisance and a danger as they could fall and hurt themselves. It was hard to stop them, though, as they were the children of our neighbours and friends. My father had a mechanic fix a wire to the magneto. When the switch was turned on, anyone touching the car from the outside would get a mild electric shock. As the children were barefoot, they were very vulnerable. After a few shocks, they stopped taking their free rides. Soon we were able to drive past without anyone jumping aboard.

Even when it rained, we had lots of fun playing and frolicking in the rain. Truly, it rains "cats and dogs" in the tropical thunderstorms in Singapore. Lighting would zap across the sky, followed by thunderclaps loud enough to split open the heavens. Often we jumped with fright as the thunder seemed to clap right beside us. Rain would pour down in buckets, and everyone would run into the house for shelter. But not us children. Mother was kind enough to let us play in the rain in the cement courtyard of our house. While the older folks watched, I would jump, cavort, sing, and play about with my sister Geok, all soaking wet and so happy in the rain. When the rain stopped, and it was all over in less than thirty minutes, we had a bath, changed into dry clothes, and had warm soup.

Chinese New Year was something we children looked forward to every year. On New Year's Eve, the house was swept clean, and everything was put in its proper place. It was considered bad luck to use a broom on New Year's Day, as one would sweep all the luck away. The house was spic and span, and Mother and my sisters were all busy cooking. We would have a family feast on New Year's Eve.

On New Year's Day, we dressed in new clothes, and we children wished our parents "Happy New Year" (*sin ni kuai lok*). When we did so, they gave us red packets (*ang pau*) with some money inside. On the second day until the fifteenth day, (Chinese New Year celebrations last for fifteen days), we visited relatives and close friends, and in turn, received guests at our home. It was tradition to bring an even number of oranges as gifts when visiting, and to serve cakes and sweetmeats when receiving guests. In either case, there were always *ang paus* for the children.

I was overjoyed when I was given a small packet of firecrackers. They were small ones, about an inch long, thin like matches, and came in a string of about ten to fifteen pairs joined at the fuses. The noise they made, though slight, was the most delightful sound to my boyhood ears.

I soon ventured into playing with bigger ones. These were about three inches long, pencil-thick, and about ten in a packet. I separated them and, holding one, lit its fuse with a burning joss stick and threw it high in the air where it exploded with a bang. I would also put them one at a time under a cigarette tin. When the cracker exploded, the tin went sailing in the air. Good fun!

I became braver and would hold one end of a firecracker with the tip of my fingers, light it, and let it explode while still holding on. I even tried this with one of the giant crackers that were about an inch thick. This caused a numbing sensation in my fingers, but it was worth it as all my playmates said I was so brave.

One day, my father heard about what I was doing, and I received one of the worst scoldings I ever had from him. If my mother had heard, I would surely have received a caning from her. That put a stop to my firecracker feats. I was lucky my fingers were not blown off by such foolishness.

Later, after I started school, Father began to sell earth excavated from the other hill on the estate. He sometimes asked me to record the number of lorries that drove by on the road below our house. Sitting on the side of the culvert that drained the wastewater from our house, I jotted down the number of lorries that went by. Father gave me 2c for every lorry that I counted. He must have sold thousands of lorry-loads of red earth from the hill, although the hill seemed hardly dented. Sometimes, I also followed Father on his rounds to collect rent from the people who had built their houses on his estate. He usually gave me some money from the rent he collected, and I spent the money buying tops and kites.

When the "top season" came, tops of all sizes and shapes appeared. All of them were made of wood (I don't think there was much plastic around at that time). Some were coloured red, yellow, or green, and some were just unpainted plain wood. Now was the chance for us boys to show off our collection of tops. We checked that the screws that served as the stems of the tops were screwed in tightly, and practised spinning our tops. To spin a top, we first wound a quarter-inch thick cord around the stem; then, we threw the top to the ground while pulling on the cord to give the top a spin.

A man with a cart came along to our village, selling tops of all kinds and shapes. Some were slender, some were fat, some were egg-shaped, and some looked like small turnips. I bought a slender one that was heavy for its size and another that was like a turnip, low and round with a screw cut off at one end for the stem.

We played with our tops on the road. Very soon, we were competing to see how long our tops could spin. My turnip top was unbeatable. Time and again, it would spin and spin without stop, beating all the others. Sometimes, as it was spinning, I would pull on the cord to lift it up from the ground onto my palm. Or I would throw it and catch it to spin on my hand instead of on the ground. Everyone was envious of my turnip top. They did not know that I had chosen it because it was low and heavier at the bottom and so could spin a long time without wobbling or toppling over.

We often had top battles, in which we smashed tops against each other, trying to dent or knock away our opponents' tops. Some of us could spin the top in such a way that its stem would strike and dent the opponent's top. Sometimes the top that was hit would break into pieces, and we would all have a good laugh. Using my slender top, I soon became an expert in denting, hitting, and displacing other tops. I had chosen the slender top because it was heavy. It was made of hardwood. Softwood is lighter and easily dented or broken.

What a wonderful time we had playing with tops. It was such good fun that sometimes I was late coming home for dinner. I knew I was in trouble then. My mother used to wait at the steps of the house with a cane, and I had to pass her to go up into the house. I tried to run quickly, but she always managed to give me a few swipes on the legs. Oh, that was painful. But it taught me a lesson: come back in time for dinner, or get punished.

"*Angin datang, angin datang!*" (The wind is coming, the wind is coming!) When this cry was heard, a wave of excitement swept through the *kampong* (village) close to our house. All the Malay children went searching for their kites. I looked for mine but could not find it anywhere. To join in the fun, I hurriedly took a piece of paper, the size of an exercise book, and folded the two longer ends in about an inch. I pierced a hole ¾ inch from the top through each folded margin, and passed a short string (about eight inches long) through the holes, knotting both ends to keep the string in place. To the middle of this short string, I attached a ball of string. I now had a simple makeshift kite. I took it out, running with the wind in my face. The breeze caught my kite, and it floated up and up. I was happy to see it flying in the sky.

As I grew older, I did a lot more kite flying in the fields around the house. I did not use my first kite, that simple piece of folded paper, as it was not strong enough. Running with it when there was little breeze, I was able to fly it without much effort, but it collapsed when there was a stronger wind. I bought a kite for 2c from the shop down from our house and enjoyed flying it for days.

Ahmad, the *kebun*, taught me how to make stronger kites. Taking two thin bamboo sticks, one about 12 inches (short) and the other about 16 inches (long), he tied the sticks together, the short one in the middle and the longer one about three-quarter way up, forming a cross. He connected the ends of the sticks with a string to make a frame. He placed the frame on thin kite paper and trimmed the paper along the frame with a half inch margin all round. Then he folded and pasted the margin over the strings, turning the paper and sticks into a kite. To this kite, he tied the string that would allow him to fly the kite. As this string controlled the flying abilities of the kite, this was a crucial step.

Soon I had made several kites, some square, some long and oblong, some with fanciful heads and tails. I even made a kite with sound. I tied a reed across the kite, and when it flew and soared in the sky, the wind blowing past the reed created a sound that was heard by all. Everyone rushed out to see what was making the sound. It was the sweetest music to my ear.

Kite fighting was very popular in those days. My rectangular kite would only fly steadily up into the sky and hover up there with its tail trailing and swaying below. I had to find a kite that could move around quickly in the air. I found that a diamond-shaped kite was the best. Such a kite was very agile and could even turn cartwheels in the sky. However, as it would not keep still, it needed some skill to fly. I spent hours flying it, turning it to the left and right, sending it zooming up and down and across the sky, practising all the movements I needed for kite fighting.

I searched all over our garden for broken pieces of glass and pounded the pieces I collected into powder in my mother's mortar bowl. Then I mixed the powdered glass with rice-glue or starch (used in those days to stiffen clothes after washing). Stretching my kite line between poles, I rubbed the glue with the powdered glass onto the strings. Once the sun dried the glue, the kite string was very sharp and ready for fighting.

We would signal to one another whenever we wanted a fight. Then our kites would be chasing each other across the sky. I developed a slicing attack. I would send my kite across the sky towards my opponent's, and when my string crossed his, I would draw my kite in sharply so that my kite string cut his like a knife. It worked. Often, my attack sent the other kite floating loose, its string cut. If my opponent was the aggressor and his kite string crossed mine, I would let out my string to slide along his, unharmed. Often, pulling in the string or letting it out quickly, my fingers were cut by the powdered glass on the string. Caught up with the thrill of the game, I did not mind.

When one of the kites was finally cut loose and sent floating away, the children watching the fight would go chasing after the downed kite, shouting all the way, tripping over stones, jumping across ditches, and scrambling to be the first to get it. It was really fun and exciting.

One day, I wanted to fly the highest kite in the sky—a kite so high that it would stay in the sky all day, and overnight, too. I bought several balls of string and joined them together. The string must have been over 800 feet long. I made a large kite with colourful side streamers and a long tail. I asked one of my playmates to hold the kite with its head up. Running fast while pulling the string, I launched the kite into the sky.

As the kite climbed up into the air, I let the string out until there was no more, and the kite was a mere spot in the sky. The kite flew steadily in the sky for hours, at times soaring like an eagle. Towards the evening, I tied the string to a bush and left it overnight. However, when I returned the next morning, the string was broken. The kite was gone. It had flown away. It had gone beyond my furthest dreams, and was roaming the skies and the heavens. I had indeed flown the highest kite of all...

Birds and Fish

IT is said, "God loved the birds and created trees; Man loved the birds and invented cages." One day, a neighbour called me to her home, and to my surprise, she gave me a small bird, a Java sparrow, in a square wooden cage. I was thrilled. I took it home with care. This started my hobby of keeping birds.

The sparrow was the most beautiful bird, blue in colour, with two white patches on each cheek. Already tame, it was not afraid of me. I was captivated by the bird hopping, chirping, and sometimes breaking into short song. Its food was simple, only *padi* (unhusked rice grains) and water, and occasionally some coarse sand or crushed shell to aid its digestion. The bird would pick up a *padi* with its beak, crack it, letting the husk drop, and swallow the rice. Then it would sip from the water cup in the cage, and start its hopping and singing all over again.

When I caught it to give it a bath, it nipped me, and I nearly had to let it go. My neighbour taught me how to put water and *padi* into the cage with a spoon from the outside, without having to open the cage. She also taught me how to draw out the tray at the bottom of the cage and change the newspaper lining when it was soiled with bird droppings.

I learned later that these sparrows were considered pests by rice farmers. Later, I also saw Chinese fortune-tellers with Java sparrows as their "assistants." When a client came, the fortune-teller would open the cage, and the trained sparrow would hop out and pick up with its beak a slip of paper from the many littered in front of the cage. The fortune-teller would take the paper from the bird, wait for it to hop back into the cage, then shut the cage. Inscribed on the piece of paper was the client's fortune, which the fortune-teller would read out loud.

One day, while passing the gardener's house, I heard a bird calling, *ter-ku-ku*. I looked about and saw a bird on a perch in an "open cage" hanging from the eaves of the house. It was like a small dove, pale brown in colour with a black patch and some white on the back of its neck. I wondered why it did not fly away from the "open cage," a cage frame with a bottom and a perch, but with all other bars removed. Hassan, the gardener's son, took down the cage and showed me that the bird's leg was tied to a short leash attached to the perch. The bird could move freely from one end to the other of the cage but could not fly away.

The bird was a cuckoo, named after its call, *ter-ku-ku*. This call sounded as though the bird was calling for the *Tengku*, the Prince, in Malay. I have heard that because of its song, the cuckoo was a protected songbird in Malaya, and that the Sultan of Johore had banned the keeping of this bird in Johore. I spent many hours learning how to cup my hands and imitate its call.

I had often seen cuckoos in open areas on the ground. They were not shy and would only fly away at the last moment when I came near. Most people preferred to keep them in "open cages," one leg tied to the perch. A newly-caught bird tied to a perch would attempt to fly away but after a few unsuccessful tries, would be resigned to its fate.

I liked the call of the cuckoo as it could be heard from a distance. I bought a bird and a cage with all the fittings (a perch and cups for food and water) from one of the Malays on our estate for a special price of five dollars. After some time, it would call whenever I walked past or was close to it.

Hassan had another bird, a *merbok*, that he kept in a circular cage. It was grayish blue, while its cheeks, crown and nape were brownish, with a pattern of small crescent-shaped bars. It was about half the size of a pigeon, much smaller than the cuckoo. Its food was a smaller type of *padi*. Its call went *b-r-r—bo-bo-bo-bo*. The starting notes were soft and the *bo-bo-bo* got stronger and stronger after each note. Some birds had short calls, while others had long. The birds with long, strong calls were known as *kong*. I don't exactly know the meaning of *kong*, but it was meant to indicate a champion.

There are rings on the legs of the *merbok*, and it is the belief among bird fanciers that birds with an uneven number of rings would have longer calls. Birds that had thirty-three or thirty-nine rings on their legs were prized, as it was believed they would be *kong*.

I bought a *merbok* with thirty-nine rings on its legs. Excited, I counted the rings again and again in case I had made a mistake. I hoped its calls would be long and strong. Month after month, I waited for its call but it was silent. When I had almost given up on it as a dumb bird, I heard a soft call one morning. It was the start of many calls to come. The call grew stronger a day by day, until one day the Malays proclaimed it a *kong*.

I was so happy that using pulleys, I hung the cage on the highest pole in our garden, so that the bird could be heard all over the neighbourhood. Its song was admired by all.

One morning, however, it was silent. I discovered the cage was empty. A hawk must have heard its call, broken into the cage, and eaten the bird. That was a very sad ending for my champion bird. It put a stop to my bird keeping for many years.

After a time, however, I fell in love with the melodious song of the *mata puteh* ("white eyes" in Malay). This was a green wren, smaller than the sparrow, with white circles around the eyes. I got one, and fed it with bits of egg, bread, and greens, and occasionally, caught small grasshoppers for it. (Some

Malay boys were catching grasshoppers with nets and selling them at a price of two grasshoppers for 1c, but I preferred to catch my own.) I put the small grasshoppers, three or four together, in a special cage slightly smaller than a cigarette box, and hung it on the side of the birdcage. The bird would poke its beak through the bars of the cage and peck at the soft abdomen of the grasshoppers, pulling pieces away to eat. The grasshoppers did not seem to mind, as they kept on living for quite a long while without their abdomens. The *mata puteh* also loved to pick at lettuce and cucumbers.

Every week I refilled the dish of water in the cage. You should have seen how the bird enjoyed bathing itself. After dipping in, it would preen itself and sing many beautiful songs, so happy and thankful for the bath.

My Malay friends taught me how to snare birds with a noose made of horse hair, but I didn't catch any as I was too busy looking after my birds and had no time to set the snares up properly.

I guess I was lucky to have had so many hobbies when I was young. I was introduced to many of them by Hassan, the gardener's son.

One day, I visited Hassan at his home not far from our house. He took me inside and showed me a row of wide-mouthed bottles on a shelf. The bottles were half-filled with water and in each one, there was a beautiful fish. Paper dividers separated each bottle from the one beside it. When Hassan removed one of the dividers, I was fascinated to see the fish in the neighbouring bottles flaring their tails and turning deeper in colour. The two fish kept on trying to charge each other in their separate bottles, working themselves into a rage and creating a lot of foam at the surface of the water. It was an exciting sight.

Hassan wanted to give one of his fighting fish to me, but I declined, as I knew how precious they were to him. But I wanted some too. I asked him how I could get them. He told me that he had caught the fish from the pond using a rattan basket, a *pun-ki* in Hokkien. This basket is shaped like a shell, and is about 2 x 1½ feet across, and about a foot at its deepest. There are handles on both side of the basket. I had seen men using this basket to carry earth from the side of the hill to load onto lorries.

I decided to catch some fighting fish for myself. The next day, in my customary singlet and blue shorts, and barefoot as usual, I took one of the many rattan baskets lying around our house, and with a large bottle half filled with water tied around my waist, I went to the pond. I must have looked a sight, rather like a child labourer than the son of a reputable landlord.

Using the basket as a scoop, I plunged it into the clear water and drew it up. Water drained out of the basket through the rattan weave. I was disappointed to see nothing of interest in the basket. I tried time and time again without success. I thought I must be doing it wrong. I scooped at some plants with long, trailing, furry roots floating in the water. This time, I got some rainbow fish and tetras, but as they were not the fighting fish I wanted, I threw them all back into the water.

I tried again and again, until finally, I saw some fighting fish jumping in the basket after I had drawn it up from the water. What a joy I felt. I picked the fish up gently from the basket, put them into my bottle, and headed home. There, I filled some empty jam jars with water from the large earthenware water jar in the house, and put one fish in each. I then inserted paper dividers between the jars.

Among the fighting fish that I had caught, there were a few rather stout ones with smaller fins. They seemed plain and did not look very fierce. Again from Hassan, I learned that these were females, and that I should keep them if I wanted to breed fighting fish. He told me to put some water plants in the water to make the fish feel more at home, and to keep the jars away from sunlight so that the water would be cool and comfortable for the fish.

Now I had to learn how to feed them. Hassan taught me how to catch the tiny worms that could be found in certain parts of the stream. I also searched for mosquito larvae, breeding in open cracks and small puddles around the house.

After a week or so, the water in the jars was getting cloudy and foul with waste matter. It was time to change the water. I poured the water and fish in a basin, and after rinsing the jars several times, filled them partially with fresh water from the water jar in our house. I added some of the floating water plants with the furry tails. Then I caught the fish gently in my hand and transferred them back into their jars. The water was from our well, and it was pure, with no chemicals added. (Our tap water today has chlorine in it and will kill the fish unless the water is left exposed overnight to clear the chlorine.)

One day Hassan asked, "Do you want to make your fish fiercer and better fighters?" Under his guidance, I took some plump, ripe chillies from my mother's vegetable basket in the kitchen, and after sprinkling water on them, kept them in a cool place. After some days, I saw worms squirming and wriggling in the chillies. As they grew chubby and fat, I picked up some with a toothpick and dropped them in the jars. With a sudden flourish, the fighting fish caught the worms in their mouths and gobbled them up with relish. They must be fond of such real hot stuff!

Soon, I had quite a few fighting fish lined up on the shelf. Once, I had some in some wide-mouthed bottles. The next morning, the bottles were still there, but the fish were gone. I thought the lizards had come during the night and fished them out with their tails. I told Hassan and was a little upset when he laughed. He said, "Fighting fish like to jump, especially when there is bright light from the moon or a lamp above. Cover the bottles with cloth if you don't want to lose them again." (He suggested cloth as it, being porous, would allow the water to "breathe.") I had learned another valuable lesson from experience and from Hassan.

I liked to see the fish flaring up and their colours growing brilliant when I removed the paper dividers. Sometimes, I would place a mirror next to a bottle. On seeing its reflection in the mirror, the fish would instantly swim to fight against its own image. On several occasions, I saw real fights, with two fish in the same bottle. They were ferocious, going at each other with no holds barred. They snapped at each other, and locked together at the mouth, wove and thrust in the water with all their might. Sometimes, when they were evenly matched, both fish would float and rest for a bit, exhausted from fighting. After a while, they would resume their battle. Otherwise, they would not stop until either one of them turned tail and, pale all over, swam away to hide in the trailing water plants, or until one died in the fight and its body floated to the top of the water.

I really did not like to see them fighting. Their tails and fins got so tattered and torn, and their bodies so damaged and bruised, with bites all over. They looked battered and dismal after a fight. To let them recover, I put their bottles in a dark place where the fish could rest until their fins grew back to their former shape. After a while, I seldom let them at each other in the same bottle. I would simply enjoy watching them display aggressively in their separate bottles when I removed the paper divider.

I learned many years later that Singapore fighting fish have round fins, while the Siamese variety have bigger and more fanciful tails. The tails of some Siamese fish are up to three or four inches long. But such trailing tails are extra targets that suffer much damage during a fight.

Fighting fish need very little space and can be kept in a small glass container. They are a feast for the eyes, resplendent in their colours of red, green, blue, and some even black, with their fins flowing majestically as they swim. They live about four to five years and need little care. They are omnivorous and easy to feed. The cost of keeping them is so little, but the pleasure is so great. Their name, *Betta splendens*, is an apt name for such beautiful creatures.

Crocodiles, Tigers, and Flying Foxes

MY brothers were fond of swimming. We would secretly go to swim in a pond about half a mile from our house. As Mother had forbidden us to swim, we had to go into the water naked so that our clothes were dry when we got home. Otherwise, we would have got a caning from her.

One day, my brother took me on the back of his bicycle to Tampines,[13] about five miles from our house. We enjoyed ourselves swimming in the creek there, back and forth among the mangrove trees. A few days later, we heard that that someone had seen a crocodile in that very same creek. We were too scared to go there again to swim.

I had five brothers, and the three older ones had guns and were fond of hunting. On hearing the story, they wanted to hunt for the crocodile. Together with some friends, they went several times with their guns to the mangrove creek but did not see the crocodile. One day, one of their friends tried a different method. He waded into the water and splashed about, hoping that the crocodile would hear him and swim out to look for food. After some time, the others saw a movement in the water some distance away and shouted to him to get out quickly. True enough, the crocodile appeared. The men scrambled away to safety.

People who knew told my brothers that their shotguns were too weak to kill the crocodile. The bullets would just bounce off its thick hide. A very high-powered rifle was needed, and they didn't have it. So they had to think of something else.

The next day, they set a trap. One of them got into the water to splash about, and the crocodile appeared again. Somehow, they caught it, tied it up, and brought it to our house. It took many men to capture it. All the neighbours came to have a look. The tail measured some six feet, and the jaws were two feet long and full of razor-sharp teeth. All in all, the crocodile was about ten feet long. It was a fearsome, powerful reptile.

We had to call our uncle again, the one who had cut and skinned the python. He had a Chinese medicine shop and was a taxidermist, an expert in skinning animals, stuffing and mounting them, especially reptiles and birds. We watched at a distance as he killed the crocodile. As he was skinning it, the crocodile suddenly opened its mouth and lashed out with its tail. We all had a fright and ran away.

---

[13] Spelt "Tampinis" or "Tampenis"at that time. There was much talk when the government changed the spelling in later years.

Our uncle told us later that he must have touched a motor nerve as he was skinning the crocodile. Although the crocodile was dead, touching the nerve had set off a reflex action, causing the jaws to open and the tail to move. Our uncle gave us some of the crocodile meat, but when we cooked it, it had a very fishy smell, so we did not eat it. We threw the meat away.

We never went back to the creek to swim again, as there might have been other crocodiles waiting for us. We were lucky to have escaped the first time.

My brothers told me they would bring me along on their next hunting trip in the jungle during the weekend. I was so excited that the night before we set out, I dreamt of encounters with tigers, wild pigs, deer, lynx, monkeys, and snakes, all in an adventure like the *Jungle Book* stories.

Morning came, and I got ready to follow my brothers on their hunting trip. Some sandwiches and a water bottle were put in a small backpack for me to carry. Later on, I realized they were for me—my brothers were afraid I might get hungry or thirsty in the jungle. With two Malay friends as guides, my two brothers and myself, there were five of us. I was told I had to be quiet, and that if they were shooting, to squat down so that I would not be in their way.

We went down single file along a small trail that led us deeper and deeper into the jungle. I saw monkeys swinging about in the trees and squirrels jumping from branch to branch. I also saw small lizards on some branches and birds high in the treetops. Although it was day, it was dark, and sometimes we had to brush aside the undergrowth or bend to walk under branches. We walked and walked until we reached a small clearing where there was a running stream. Here, we waited at a distance from the water.

We waited for some time. Whenever there was a rustle in the undergrowth, we all tensed up, and my brothers prepared to shoot. Some small mouse deer came to drink at the stream, but my brothers did not shoot. They were waiting for a wild pig that the Malay guides had seen some days ago at this drinking hole.

Suddenly, a hush seemed to grip the whole forest. Even the birds stopped flying and singing. "*Harimau* (Tiger)," whispered one of the guides, and we too fell quiet. There was a movement in the undergrowth, and suddenly, the tiger appeared.

It took a look in our direction, then quickly disappeared in the forest. I was quite shaken by the experience. We waited again for some time, but nothing appeared. I think the animals knew the tiger was around and so were keeping away as much as they could.

So ended my first hunting trip.

Our Malay friends told us they were surprised by the appearance of the tiger. There had been talk among their people about a tiger in the vicinity, but our friends were sceptical and did not expect to see it.[14] They had only led us to shoot the wild pig. My brothers too, were surprised and scared. Their guns, 12 gauge double-barrelled shotguns, would not have been powerful enough to kill a tiger.

Afterwards, there were rumours of one or two more glimpses of the tiger, but after that, it was never seen again. It had disappeared deep into the jungle.

One of our neighbours told my brother that a panther had been raiding their chickens at night. So we set forth one night to hunt it, armed with long torches and a shotgun. We were walking along some rambutan trees, shining our torchlights here and there, when suddenly we heard some movement in the trees. We turned around and pointed our torchlights up at the trees. To our surprise, we saw a boy in the trees, plucking (stealing) rambutans. It gave us a fright as we might have shot him. We told him never to climb trees and pluck rambutans in the night again.

We walked on and suddenly, in a distant tree, we saw two bright eyes reflecting our torchlight beam. There was a big cat in the tree. My brother shot at it, and it fell with a big bump. It was a panther about four feet long—three or four times the size of a big cat. Our neighbour was very happy that his chickens and pigs were now safe.

Rambutan season was one of the best times for me. These delicious, red and hairy-skinned fruit (*rambut* in Malay means "hair") came into season twice a year. My father had several rambutan trees, and our immediate neighbour had more. When the fruit ripened, I would climb our trees and eat and eat rambutans almost everyday. One day, trying to reach a particular juicy bunch,

---

[14] Editor's note: This episode about the tiger excited some debate among family members, some of whom were adamant about tigers being extinct in Singapore, even at the time of my father's childhood (the late twenties). One legend holds that the last tiger in Singapore was shot at the Raffles Hotel in 1904. However, a book put out by Singapore's Oral History Department, *Recollections, People and Places* (1990), reports the shooting of a tiger in Choa Chu Kang in 1930, and a recent Web site (www.frommers.com) listed 1932 as the date the last tiger was shot in Singapore. As recently as 1997, there were reports of a tiger on Pulau Ubin, one of the islands outlying Singapore. It has been speculated that tigers could have swum over to Singapore from Malaysia.

I "over-climbed." The branch broke, and I fell about twelve feet to the ground with a thud. I could not walk properly for a few days. The incident taught me a valuable lesson: never be too greedy.

At night, huge bats called flying foxes would fly in from Mandai and the Johore forests to feast on the rambutans as well. Their leathery wings had a span of three to five feet, and they had sharp claws, sharp teeth, and bodies covered with dark red fur. The bats made screeching sounds as they fought each other for the best fruit. If they were not kept off, they would eat up all the rambutans on a tree in a night or two.

My brothers were often invited back home to shoot the flying foxes. Happily, I was also allowed to tag along. My job was to search for the flying foxes that had been shot, and to collect them. My brothers preferred to shoot the flying foxes as they were in the air circling the trees. Once the bats got on the trees, they would cling to the branches even after they had been shot, and we could not easily get them off. I spent a lot of time enjoying rambutans while my brothers waited for the flying foxes to come.

Usually, after we had shot two or three, we took them home. My mother would skin them, and adding some Chinese herbs, ginger and black soya sauce, cook them the next day into a delicious soup for all of us. It makes my mouth water when I think of those days...

| Mother reading the Bible (post-war photo) | Father in the front of the house, June 2, 1946 |

My parents, Lim Teck Boo and Giam Cheng Kiat, and me, on my wedding day, November 24, 1950

My sisters, around 1925. *From left*: Soon Geok, Soon Bian, Soon Suat. *In front:* Soon Teck.

The Lim brothers, around 1934. *Back row, from left*: Siew Tee, Siew Poh (myself), Siew Boon. *Front row, from left*: Siew Ek, Siew Guan, Siew Hui.

Anglo-Chinese School (Coleman Street) boys in the school playground, 1935. The tiffin shed is in the background.

Myself, in front of a British pillbox (post-war photo). These concrete pill-boxes were built to defend Singapore's eastern and western coasts.

Myself, in 1948

Clifford Pier, probably in the late fifties or early sixties (Photo by author)

A *sampan*. This picture, taken in 1970, shows a commercial boat used for ferrying goods or passengers. The *sampan* in which my brother-in-law and I went fishing could only carry two people. (Photo by author)

The area around our family home on the coconut estate, July 2006. Lim Teck Boo Road has been transformed into a heavily built-up area, in which construction is now underway to build a Mass Rapid Transit (MRT) station for the Circle Line. (Photo by C. Lim)

Kim Chuan Road, July 2006. This area has also been affected by the construction of the MRT station for the Circle Line. (Photo by C. Lim)

Schooldays

My turn at ACS

WHEN we were living at the bungalow on Kim Chuan Avenue, my mother, busy in the house, often told me to ride in the horse-drawn carriage that took my brothers and sisters to school and back. The driver sat high up in his seat, and we children squeezed in the carriage behind, slightly below him. I enjoyed riding in the carriage, hearing the reins jingling and the horses going *clip clop* along the way.

When I returned home from the ride, though, the house was empty and quiet without my siblings. Lonely, and with no one to play with, I waited for their return. When they came home, they showed me their schoolbooks with many pictures, and I became fascinated with the idea of going to school. "One day, you will go to school also," said my sisters and brothers. I longed for the day when I could attend school like them.

However, it was only after we moved to Father's new house on the rubber estate that I was old enough to start school. At six years of age, I entered the Anglo-Chinese School (ACS) on Coleman Street. My brothers had studied at ACS as well, and it had a name as the best mission school at that time. We were sent to be educated in English because knowing English was an advantage in getting a job in Singapore then (study of Chinese at that time was not considered important).

In preparation, my sister sewed some new shorts and shirts for me, and my brother bought me a pair of canvas shoes ("rubber shoes," we called them) from Bata. I was shown how to apply white shoe polish (blanco) on the canvas so that the shoes looked neat and clean.

Early one Monday morning, dressed in white shirt, blue shorts, canvas shoes, and with hair neatly combed, I followed my brother to take the bus to school. This was my first time taking the bus, and it was all new to me. I was not accustomed to wearing shoes as I had been running barefoot most of my childhood days.

We arrived at the school on Coleman Street. I was amazed to see so many boys of my age, and many who were older. This was indeed a big world, with so many other boys of all ages. I looked forward to making friends and playing with them. We all assembled at a large playground on top of a hill and formed into rows. A woman teacher herded a group of us down the steps to our classroom. We were each assigned to a small desk with an attached chair. In awe of my teacher, I listened carefully to each and every of her words. I was not in the least afraid, as my brother Siew Tee was in the same school in a higher grade, and he had told me that he would come to take me home after school.

Anglo-Chinese School on Coleman Street consisted of three buildings built on the slope of Fort Canning Hill. On the lower part of the slope was a three-storey building that held the classes for the first two years (Primary I and Primary II, as we called them). There were three classes for each year, the A, B, and C classes, and an occasional D class. The Primary I classes were on the lower floor while the Primary II classes had the higher floors. Higher up the slope was another three-storey building occupied by the Standard 1 to Standard V students, again divided in classes A, B, and C, and the occasional D. Between these two buildings was a large hall with a stage and a piano. The hall was used for singing and drama classes, and as a chapel for service on Monday or Friday mornings.

On top of the hill was the large playground, used for drill, games, and annual events. At one end of the playground was the tiffin shed, a large shed with many tables and benches. During recess, hawkers sold food and snacks at the tables, and students sat on the benches while eating. The shed was also the gathering place for all the *amahs* (housemaids) that accompanied boys to school. Sheltered steps led from each building up the hill to the recess area. Those in the buildings lower down the hill had to climb many more steps than those further up.

I remember well my early days in school. Each morning, after lining up outside, we were led to our classroom to sit at our desks. The top of the wooden desks could be lifted, and bags, books and pencils kept inside. The forty students in the class sat in rows facing the teacher and a huge blackboard on the wall.

After a roll call, we began our lessons. Our first lessons were on the alphabet. We nervously gripped our HB pencils as we copied the letters A to Z, in capitals, in our exercise books. Unlike the children of present days, I had never held a pencil and did not know how to write before going to school, I had never held a pencil before I went to school. The teacher looked at our work and gave us marks. Those who received more than 80 marks were happy, while those who received poor marks were ashamed and tried to hide their books.

At times, the teacher showed us picture cards, telling us the names of the things shown in the pictures, and drilling us on the proper pronunciation. She would shuffle the cards and show them again, one by one. We quickly raised our hands if we remembered the names. We all wanted to be first and hoped the teacher would call us to name the objects in the picture.

Then suddenly, the recess bell would sound. On being dismissed, we ran up the steps to the tiffin shed. We had only a fifteen- to twenty-minute break and had to make the best of it.

There was usually a stampede for the popular food, and long and busy lines formed at the stalls selling *kway teow* (a type of flat noodles) and *mee goreng* (fried noodles). It was less crowded at the stalls selling ice water and *kachang puteh* (roasted chick peas, but also a general term for roasted and fried salted nuts, beans and peas). Having only a few cents in my pocket, I usually headed for the *kachang puteh* seller. Seeing me, he would fill and give me a paper cone full of the appetising *kachang puteh*, still warm to the touch. As I was his regular customer, he sometimes added a handful more as a bonus. He also had peanut *goreng* (fried peanuts) and soft, boiled *kachang kudah* (chick peas), but I liked *kachang puteh* best of all. What more of a meal could one buy for one cent!

After recess, the teacher taught a variety of subjects with small breaks in between. We learned writing, reading, spelling, and arithmetic. We had to learn the times-tables (multiplication tables) by heart. The teacher tested us orally on spelling each week, and those who could not spell correctly had to stand in the corner as punishment.

Then there were singing classes and drill. These were not so popular. One year, the teacher planned to put on a play at the end of term. I was chosen for the part of a girl and had to learn how to curtsy. On top of that, I had to wear a dress. All my friends teased me mercilessly. Try as I would, the teacher would not let me change my part. I was so ashamed that on the day of the performance, I absented myself from school on the excuse that I was sick. The play was performed without my part.

Storytelling was the most interesting subject. The teacher read a chapter from a book each week. We listened raptly to exciting stories of Aladdin and his magic lamp, and Ali Baba and the forty thieves, anxious to hear the next chapter.

Every week, there was a period for chapel. Sometimes, when we forgot to bring our hymnbook (*Hymns of the Kingdom*), we tried to sneak past the teacher, carrying a small book in its place. Invariably, the teacher would catch us. Then we had to stay back after school to write a few hundred lines of "I must not forget to bring my hymnbook on chapel days."

Most of my friends bought new textbooks for school, but I mostly inherited my brothers' and sisters' old books. If they did not have the ones I needed, we went scouring the second-hand bookshops on Bras Basah Road for them.

My old books often had my brothers' and sisters' notes written in them, and they helped me in my schoolwork.

Schooling was fun, and I made many friends. My earliest friend in Primary School was Chng Kiat Leng. Kiat Leng's parents were very rich, and he used to go to school with an *amah* up to Standard V (when he was thirteen years old). She waited for him in the tiffin shed during school hours. She even put a bib on him when he ate. Everyone used to tease him except me.

Somehow, he liked me, and when we were older, he often brought me to his house on Neil Road and gave me his comics and magazines after he had read them (I was too poor and could not afford to buy any). The magazines featured all sorts of articles and gadgets of boyish interest that fascinated me. I read eagerly his copies of *Film Fun* and *Hotspurs*, and learned all I could about Charles Atlas, hockey, and boxing.

After the war, he completed a degree in London, and then went on to Harvard to study law, graduating *cum laude*. As far as I know, he never worked in a law office (he was too rich to have to do so), but he was very respected in government circles. He had a brilliant mind and was somewhat eccentric in his ways. He never married. Sadly, he was found dead in his flat one day.

Another one of my friends was Chek Joon Woon, who sold me his Hercules Sports bicycle on a three-year instalment plan. As schoolboys and at such a young age, we entered into a long-term business transaction based on friendship and mutual trust, and we completed it without any setback.

Then there was Tan Joo Liang. Tall and lanky, and brilliant in his studies, he received straight As in his Cambridge exams.[15] I often played badminton at his house in Newton. He became a doctor and had a clinic on Makepeace Road, off Bukit Timah Road. It was sad news when he collapsed and died at his clinic—a good man lost at an early age.

I also met at school the flamboyant Wong Peng Tuck, son of a distinguished family in Singapore. We later went to Manila together as representatives for the Singapore Jaycees. He became a lawyer who led a colourful life.

Last, but not least, is my good friend, Wee Teow Kee. We were friends from Primary 1 onwards, right through to the end of school. He became a devout member of the Salvation Army, and his backstroke won him many swimming awards. During the Japanese regime, we often cycled together to the house of his friend, Peter Lim, in Katong, where we listened for hours to Peter's collection of vinyl classical records played with a pine needle. Teow Kee's love for oration and singing led him to perform in many recitals.

---

[15] Students then took examinations set by Cambridge University in England. The examination papers were sent by ship to England to be marked.

There were many others whose lives crossed mine and left their mark. We remained friends for years even after we finished school. In 1950, all three classes of the ACS Senior Class of 1941 started meeting annually on April 1st for dinner (the April Fools' Dinner). Sadly, there are barely enough of us remaining now to fill a table.

At school, I was introduced to a new world and a new way of life. I learned new things, new words, new ideas, and met new friends. Soon, most of my time was taken up with schoolwork and studies. My childhood world of pure play was gone.

Just as Eldest Sister, Soon Teck, had taken on the responsibility of supporting Second and Third Sister to study at a secondary school in Seremban, my eldest brother, Siew Guan, undertook to support me through school. It was very brotherly and generous of him as he was only a salaried man of limited means. He paid for my bus fare and school fees until I finished school. I felt indebted to him all my life for his support.

I was "shipped off" to live at his hospital quarters at Outram Road, as it was much nearer to school than our house in Paya Lebar. I needed only to take a single bus from his house to get to school. (My older brother Siew Tee soon finished school, and I took the bus by myself to school and back.)

My brother's quarters were quite small. I was given a tiny room, probably a storeroom, for myself. My sister-in-law washed and ironed all my clothes and prepared all my meals. She saw to it that I had a proper breakfast before going to school. My brother was strict, and every month I had to present him with an itemised bill for school fees, bus fare, cake money, hair cut, books, pencils, and so on. At the end of term, when my report card came, I had to show it to him to get his signature. Fortunately, it was O.K.

Brother and Sister-in-law were kind and good to me, but here at their place, I was no longer free to roam as I pleased. I felt I was a guest in their house, and I had to restrain myself and be on my best behaviour. I longed for the free and easy life I had had at the old house.

For a year or so, my parents rented a flat at Selegie Road so that my sister Geok would be nearer her school on Mount Sophia. My parents paid for someone to cook meals and look after the place, and I moved in to keep her company. The flat was within walking distance to her school, but to get to ACS, I had to take two buses, from Selegie Road to the junction of Bras Basah Road and New Bridge Road, and from there to ACS. My parents found that hiring a rickshaw to take us both to school was safer and more practical.

Daily, the rickshaw puller came to take us to school and back in his rickshaw. He was such a gentle man, and he treated me like his own dear son. He would wait patiently for me at school, hold me by the hand, and carry my bag. I thought of him as an uncle. He had great stamina and ran an easy lope, steadily, all the way, from ACS on Coleman Street, to the Methodist Girls' School on Mount Sophia, to the Selegie Road flat, a journey of about a mile and a half. Sometimes, he looked a bit gaunt to me, and I wondered whether he smoked opium during the night. When it came time for my parents to cancel the arrangement, I was sad to say goodbye. I missed him and the rides very much.

I moved to the flat of my brother Siew Hui, near Newton, for a while; then, when I was about twelve years old, my parents and brother agreed that I could return to the old house. Only my parents and my brother Siew Tee lived there now, all my other elder brothers and sisters having left to set up their own lives.

Back home, I found that I had to take care of many necessities that I had taken for granted. As I only had two shirts and two pairs of pants, I couldn't wait for the scheduled house washing and ironing, and had to do my own laundry. It meant taking my clothes to the well, scrubbing them on a washing board, rinsing and soaking them in a solution of starch (to make them stiff when dried, so that they would iron well), and hanging them up on a wire to dry in the sun. Then I had to iron them, using an iron heated by burning coals. My schedule did not match that of my parents, so I did not eat my meals with them. Instead, I helped myself to cold food left by my mother on the table or in the cupboard. I had to wake myself up early to get to school on time. However, I willingly did all these things as I felt so much freer at home.

To amuse myself, I learned how to play the mouth organ, and spent days and nights practising and playing the old songs over and over again. I learned how to cup my hands for more bass and to create a vibrato effect. I bought a Horner mouth organ with a key for sharps and flats from TMA, the music shop on High Street, and often at the Friday "program session" at school, I was called upon to entertain my classmates with my music.

I had always longed for a radio, but there was no electric power at the old house. One of my classmates told me about a crystal wireless set that required no current. I was most interested and soon bought one through mail order and learned how to build it. After that, I spent most of the evenings listening to music on the radio. There was no TV then.

Hercules

IN Standard VI, when I was fourteen, I started attending ACS at Cairnhill. Taking the bus to school was an adventure in itself. School started at 8:00 AM, and I had to allow myself more than two hours to get there on time. I began a daily routine of waking before 6:00 AM, taking a quick bath, rushing through breakfast, and walking the half mile from the house to the bus stand on Paya Lebar Road. There, I waited to catch the bus to Serangoon Road (fare 3c), where I boarded the bus going downtown, to Tekka/Kandang Kerbau (fare 6c). If I took the tram, it cost only 4c, but it was slower. From Tekka, I took a tram to Newton (3c first class, 2c second class), then walked the last half mile or so to school at Cairnhill.

The whole journey on the bus took about an hour, but I had to allow additional time for waiting. The buses were seldom punctual and were often late and full in the morning rush. Once the bus stopped, I had to quickly push ahead to get in. Sometimes, when it was too full, it would not stop, even though those waiting would wave wildly to the driver. I would then have to wait for the next bus.

It was a frantic rush to school every morning. If I was late or missed a connecting bus or tram, I had to run all the way to school from Newton so as to arrive before the bell rang. When I came home (by bus again), there was no time to think of play, as I had to do my homework. Gone were my days of leisure.

After a while, a thought came to me. Why not cycle partway to school? If I cycled from the house to Serangoon Road, it would save me both the walk from the house and the bus fare from Paya Lebar to Upper Serangoon Road, a total of 6c (3c to and fro) a day.

My brother Siew Hui made arrangements so that I could park my bicycle for the day without charge at a coffee shop at the junction of Serangoon Road and Paya Lebar Road. I was using an old, heavy gent's bike, with a 24-inch frame and regular 2½-inch rims, left over by my brothers. It was almost bigger than myself. I had to carry the bicycle all the way down the steps to the basement of the shop, and in the afternoon, haul it up again. However, I did not mind since it gave me more time to bus down to school. Best of all, I could save some money, as my brother Siew Guan kindly agreed to continue giving me the same monthly allowance for bus fare even though I was cycling part of the way.

As a special favour, the coffee shop would let me have a plate of plain rice with green curry poured over it for only 1c. For 2c, small pieces of meat were included. For 3c, the shop threw in a cup of coffee with condensed milk included. With the money saved from my allowance, I could enjoy a satisfying

curry lunch and coffee whenever I was hungry. The first time I tasted the curry
and coffee, I felt like a king having a feast. However, I dared not indulge myself
too often as I was trying to save money.

After a time, I thought I would try cycling all the way to school. It would
save me more of the monthly allowance given by my brother. Could I do it?
One Saturday, I made a trial run. The journey took about forty minutes. I cal-
culated that if I were to be on time for school, I would have to start from home
at 7.00 AM. I would have a little more time and need not rush through my
breakfast.

I felt that cycling all the way would be interesting. On my bicycle, I had
noticed many details in the shops and houses along the way—I had only seen
these buildings fleetingly from the bus. Now I could stop at any time to admire
them, and to explore. I was free to go wherever I wanted, at no extra cost. Most
important of all, I could save my entire daily bus fare of about 24c.

I decided to do it. And so, I cycled the six or seven miles to school all the
way, to and fro, for the next four years. Sometimes, with a headwind, the
cycling was twice as hard and took a longer time. Sometimes, there was rain,
but I cycled on, covering myself with a cape. I still often got soaked to the skin,
but my books were safe and dry, wrapped up in waxed paper.

Soon I became stronger, and with the bicycle, I went everywhere, to Raffles
Library at Stamford Road, to night school on Prinsep Street to study Chinese,
and to visit my friends in Katong. I enjoyed my freedom and happily saved my
money. But, as cars passed me, leaving me in their exhaust, I promised myself
that I would try to better myself when I finished school. One day, I vowed, I
would be driving a car instead of pedalling a bicycle.

The rickety old bicycle I rode was actually too big for me, but I had to use
it until I had saved enough to buy a better bicycle—a three-speed bicycle was
my aim. While visiting a classmate, Joon Woon, at his home, I saw his bicycle
and admired it very much. It was a blue Hercules, an 18-inch sports model
with three speeds and 1½-inch rims. It was a Rolls Royce compared to my
truck! Joon Woon said that as he was not using it, he would sell it to me for
$45.00. When I told him I could only afford $1.50 per month, he agreed, as a
good friend, to let me pay him in instalments over a three-year period.

I brought my new Hercules bicycle home proudly, pedalling my old bicycle
and pushing the Hercules with one hand on its handlebar. I managed to reach
home safely, although it was hard to steer two bikes at the same time, each with
just one hand. I was lucky not to be stopped or arrested. Perhaps the police in
those days were rather lenient and not so strict with boys.

My new bicycle was so light and fast that I was now able to reach school in
thirty minutes without difficulty. Changing the gears, I could ride uphill with

ease, and the headwind did not seem so strong after all. I was happy and took great care of it. It took me three years to pay my friend, but it was worth it. I used the bicycle everyday until I finished school.

Diversions

IN school, I was always hungry. During our daily twenty-minute recess, I stared with envy at the boys crowding the stalls selling *cha kway teow* (fried flat noodles), *oh luah* (oyster omelette), and noodle soup with fishballs or meatballs. I usually had 20c (my daily quota for tiffin during recess) with me, enough to buy a bowl of noodle soup with meat (5c), or *kway teow* (5c) and a drink (1c). But I was saving to make my bicycle payments, and I would only allow myself a one-cent packet of *kachang puteh* or *kachang kudah*, and occasionally, a glass of sugarcane water when I was thirsty. Sometimes when I could not resist the temptation, I bought a bowl of noodle soup, which I thought more economical than the *kway teow* (it had soup and so I did not need to buy a drink). I savoured every drop of the soup and wished that there were more.

I was very skinny and shorter than most of my classmates. One of our heroes was Charles Atlas, whose magnificent physique was featured in the magazines circulating among us schoolboys. We longed to have a body like him, and the magazines said we could. I took a lot of exercise to build up my body. We all tried, but could not achieve what we sought. The magazines also had features on how to add inches to one's height. I tried to grow taller by hanging on to branches of trees and doing pull-ups, but it did not seem to work.

It was only after I finished school, several years later, that I gradually grew in height, and my weight suddenly went up too.

One morning, on my way to school, I was surprised to see my sister Bian waving to me from a Chinese school. I turned my cycle in and learned that she was teaching and staying at the school. She asked me to come back after school. When I did, she gave me a warm welcome, with tea, biscuits and cakes. I was really touched and grateful for her love and care. She told me to drop in after school any day I wanted, and to tell her if I needed anything. After that, she often sewed and gave me shirts and shorts. I was really thankful as my clothes were rather old and worn.

Once, while having tea with her, I heard a most beautiful music. It was her husband, Siau Heng, playing the violin. I had never heard such beautiful tunes, and I sat enraptured by his masterful playing and technique. Although he ran a chauffeur and car rental business, Siau Heng also played professionally in a band. He loved music of all kinds. Seeing my interest, he offered to teach me how to play. I bought an old, cheap violin and started lessons.

At first, I spent hours just bowing up and down on open strings. First on the G string, then the D, the A, and then the E. I played scales over and over again. It was hard to get the correct pitch. Luckily, there was nobody around much at the old house to be tortured by my screeching and scraping on the violin for hours on end. Soon, I improved, and Siau Heng taught me to keep time with the foot secretly tapping out the tempo. I learned to play a few simple pieces, like Beethoven's *Minuet in G, Traumerei* and *Air on the G String*. Secretly, I played other songs and was delighted when I could play them reasonably well. When I managed to play with vibrato, I was in heaven.

In Standard V1 (when I was fourteen), we were given the option of taking either Latin, or shorthand and bookkeeping. I did not fancy either. As far as I was concerned, Latin was a dead language, and I did not want to work as a clerk. However, I knew that I needed a second language if I wanted a good Senior Cambridge certificate, so I decided to take up Chinese instead.[16] I enrolled at the Chinese School on Prinsep Street.

The only classes I could attend were in the evening. I was already attending science classes at Raffles Institution in the afternoon twice a week, so I took the Chinese classes on the same day. My Tuesdays and Thursdays now followed a strict schedule: 8:00–1:00 PM at ACS, 2:30–4:30 PM at Raffles Institution, and 5:30–7:30 PM at the Chinese School. During the hour and a half I had after ACS, I went to Raffles Library and did my homework or read books and magazines. At 4:30 PM, I made my way to Chinese School, often stopping at Waterloo Street to watch people playing football and other games. I would reach home about 8:30 PM, have a bath, take dinner, and then go to bed.

I gave up the Chinese classes after a while, as I could not cope with my schoolwork and was too exhausted to continue. During the latter part of Standard VIII, I resumed the classes, as I needed to prepare for my Senior Cambridge examinations. This time, the only available classes were on Wednesday and Friday, from 7:30–9:30 PM. Thinking of the long journey if I rode home and then back to Prinsep Street, I spent most afternoons in town, at the Raffles Library. The senior section librarian soon got to know me and often greeted me and exchanged a few words with me when I arrived.

When a hut that been used as a store next to the house became free, I asked my father to let me stay in it. I stayed in the hut during my last few years at school. Now I was like a king with my own domain. I came and went as I liked.

---

[16] Even though we spoke Hokkien, a Chinese dialect, at home, I had been educated in English and knew no Mandarin, the Chinese national language. Neither did I know how to write Chinese characters.

When hungry, I popped over to the house and ate what cooked food I found. If there was no food available, I would scrounge around for some eggs to boil. I knew I did not know how to cook and could not be bothered to try to cook other dishes.

When my sisters came, especially Bian, they would cook a whole lot of delicious dishes that I had not tasted for a long time. Then I had a gala time, gorging and savouring the food. It was like a taste of paradise, which, I knew, could not last forever.

War

The Japanese Arrive

IN 1941, the Pacific War broke out. I was seventeen and in my senior year (Standard IX) at school. We were writing our Senior Cambridge examinations when the air raid siren sounded. Following instructions, we left our papers and rushed to the air raid shelters. I think there were some who took advantage of the break to refresh their memories for the exam. When the air raid alert was over, we went back to finish our exams. It was history exams that we were writing. What a coincidence, I thought, writing history exams while history was being made with the outbreak of war.

At home, for some months past, we had had to "black out" our houses at night by covering our windows with dark cloth. Air raid wardens (mostly volunteers) went around to inspect homes to make sure no light escaped. There was an army searchlight camp on Kim Chuan Avenue near our house, and often we gathered round it, straining our necks, gazing at their searchlights sweeping the sky for enemy planes. Sometimes we heard anti-air guns firing at night.

Everywhere, there was a kind of tension in the air, and everything seemed unreal. We were told to build air raid shelters. Among the coconut trees, we dug a pit five feet deep and about six by eight feet wide. On top of the pit, Father placed stout beams of wood. He laid canvas sheeting over the beams, piled earth onto the canvas, and even planted some shrubs in the earth. He dug steps to lead down into the shelter, planting more shrubs to disguise the entrance to the steps. The shelter had some planks nailed together as seats. There was even a small pipe through the roof for ventilation. Whenever an air raid alarm sounded, we all ran to this shelter about twenty feet from our house. It could hold all of us, and we waited anxiously and quietly in it for the "all clear" siren before getting out.

My sisters and my brothers all came with their families to stay at Father's big house. They felt that the countryside was safer than the city. Our house had a huge compound (almost one acre in size), and there were many coconut trees on the estate among which they could shelter or hide if there was bombing or fighting. In the city, they had no bomb shelters in which to take refuge. The best they could do was to run down to the ground floor or hide under a table. There was also the fear that electricity and piped water would be cut. While we had no electricity, we had our well on which we could rely. During those days, those city folks who could left their houses for the countryside.

It was just as well Father had built his house with so many rooms, as so many people came to stay. There was my first brother, Siew Guan, and his wife, with their daughter, Bee Choo; my second brother, Siew Hui, and his wife; my third brother, Siew Ek and his wife; and my two other brothers, Siew Tee and Siew Boon. Three of my sisters, Soon Teck, Soon Suat, and Soon Geok, also came. Soon Bian did not come but stayed with her husband's family in Changi. Third Sister-in-law, Kah Cheng, brought her father, Reverend Tan Leng Tian, her elder sister, Kah Ann, and her younger brothers. Later, the numbers increased when more of Kah Cheng's relatives came to live on the ground floor of the house. At any one time, there were some twenty people staying at the house.

It was strange and remarkable to see so many people in the house. At mealtimes, the house was like a crowded restaurant. A sack of rice lasted only a few days, and tins of condensed milk were consumed by the dozen. Every now and then, I was asked to run to the shop to buy this or that. We bought many sacks of rice, and to prevent the rice from being eaten up by weevils, we mixed some powder (I think it was lime) with the rice. As it was cheaper and we were concerned about getting enough nutrition, we even bought unpolished rice (usually given to chickens only) for ourselves. It had a peculiar taste, but we ate it, as it was supposed to be more nutritious than polished rice.

Our home became a refuge for cars as well. Kah Cheng's younger sister, Kah Joo, and her husband, Aw Kow (son of Aw Boon Haw, the Tiger Balm founder and magnate), brought their luxury cars and parked them under the coconut trees in our compound for safety.

I had read of war in books, but having no actual experience, did not realize that wars could be so deadly. I was therefore not frightened. We heard with nonchalance that Pearl Harbour had been bombed, and that war had been declared by America on Japan. Soon it was Singapore's turn to be bombed.

Bombs fell on Boat Quay, the government offices nearby, and several places in town. I cycled to the bombed sites, and saw smashed houses and big crater-like holes in the middle of some streets. I noticed a coconut tree cut down so cleanly by bomb splinters that it seemed as if a very sharp knife had done the job. Even then, I was not afraid and did not know of the dangers that we faced. But my father knew, and was anxious to protect the family.

In one of the bedrooms upstairs, he removed a ceiling tile and strengthened the frame around it. He laid planks on top of the ceiling beams to make a platform, creating a crawl space under the roof. He made a short ladder to use for climbing up into this space. To hide the hole where the ceiling tile had been, he moved directly below it a bed with a high canopy of mosquito netting.

"When the Japanese soldiers come," he told us, "You men, try to keep the soldiers away from the room as long as possible to allow the women to hide. You women, climb onto the bed, push aside the mosquito net, move the tile away and climb up the ladder. Last person to climb, re-arrange the mosquito net, lift up the ladder, and cover up the hole. No one will dream that there are people hiding up above." The women tried out the hiding place. They climbed up above the ceiling, bringing up bottles of water and some blankets in case they needed them. It looked good and safe.

Father constructed a false wall (a sliding partition) to cover the entrance to the "secret room" in the house, and placed a tall *almeirah* (cupboard) in front. This would be another good hiding place if needed.

My sister handed me her jewels for safekeeping and asked me to hide them. I put them in a bottle, sealed it with candle wax, and buried it under one of the benches in the air raid shelter. Some of the other women buried their jewellery under the banana trees. However, after the war, they could not find their buried treasure, as the banana trees had been chopped down and new ones planted elsewhere.

The Japanese seemed to be everywhere all at once—Bangkok, Hongkong, and close to home, in the Malay peninsula. When we heard that Penang had fallen, my mother became worried for my sister, Soon Teck, who was living all alone in Seremban. The war was getting too near her town. I was sent to bring her back to Singapore.

I went to help Soon Teck pack. She wanted to leave her piano at a church in Mantin, a town some twenty-five miles north of Seremban, so I took the piano there on a lorry, even though we heard that the Japanese army were already in Kuala Lumpur, fifty miles north of Mantin. When we left Seremban for Singapore by train, there were rumbles of gunfire. A day after, Seremban fell to the Japanese. We had left just in time.

The news kept coming. *Fighting at Kluang in Johore across the causeway from Singapore. Japanese soldiers driven back at Batu Pahat. Brave Chinese volunteers made a stand for over a week. Chinese volunteers overrun.* Then, *Japanese in Bukit Timah,* just fifteen miles from our house. We saw some Australian soldiers walking through our garden to the wireless station nearby. They looked so grim and exhausted. We did not know they were retreating from the Japanese soldiers. After a few days, we heard that Singapore had fallen and surrendered.

The next morning, I looked in wonder at the womenfolk wearing shabby, dark-coloured clothes. They looked so unattractive and unkempt. Some even smelled of camphorated oil and appeared to be sick. What is the world coming to, I thought.

One day, some Japanese soldiers came to our house, and as arranged, the women fled up the ceiling and the men got busy doing different work around the house. Our dog, tied to the front of our house, began to bark at a soldier. It would not stop. The soldier gave the dog a kick but missed. He drew his sword. Smiling, I waved at the soldier to stop, and went to the dog to quieten it. Fortunately, the dog stopped barking, and the soldier sheathed his sword. He went into the house with me following at a distance, but he left without taking anything. I was young and did not know how close to danger I had been.

Soon, more soldiers came. The womenfolk again went into hiding. The soldiers found my bicycle in the loft of the chicken coop where I had hidden it under some wood. I looked helplessly as they took away my prized possession. I had lost my whole fortune. The soldiers also looted the fine cars that Kah Joo (the younger sister of Third Sister-in-law, Kah Cheng) and her husband had parked under the coconut trees in our compound. Other soldiers went into the house, and one of them saw Kah Ann, Kah Cheng's eldest sister, who was too late to go into hiding. He caught hold of her hand. She begged and begged, and all seemed lost. Suddenly, he changed his mind and let her go. Maybe it was because she looked so shabby and smelled so bad. It was a very lucky day for her.

We had all been lucky so far, but we were desperate for our safety. The womenfolk were especially very scared. We heard stories of rapes and ill treatment, and how the Japanese soldiers would shoot at random into the ceiling if they suspected people hiding above. We learned that some people had prints stamped on their hands or clothes by Japanese soldiers, and that these prints guaranteed safe transport for their bearers. We heard, too, that the Japanese were issuing safe passes for houses. How could we get one? I thought of my Japanese schoolmate, Ando, but he had left when I was in the 6th Standard. I did not know where he was. My fourth brother, Siew Tee, heard that his friend, Daniel E. Sundram, was in contact with a Japanese officer who had been in pre-war Singapore and was now a "big shot" officer in the Japanese army. Through Sundram, we managed to get a letter from the Japanese officer for our house. We showed this letter to the soldiers that came to our house, and after reading it, we were left in peace.

Father extended his vegetable garden, and soon, together with my brothers, I was helping him to plant tapioca and sweet potatoes. He also planted rows and rows of long beans and brinjals (eggplants). At the side of the garden, on the fences, he planted beans. The garden was full of vegetables. No ground was left empty.

We all tried to help Father work in the garden. Working with him, I learned much about vegetables and also the values of patience, perseverance, and responsibility. Father had endless energy and strength. Once, we were sawing up logs for firewood, my father at one end of the double-handled long saw, and my brothers, one at a time, on the other. Father and son sawed back and forth, cutting the logs. When one brother ran out of strength or breath, he would give up, and another would take his place. All the time, they kept changing shifts, but Father carried on unflagging at his end until all the wood was cut. He had outlasted them all. Afterwards, he split the log pieces further with his axe. All this was done without a word. He went on working slowly, tackling one job after another. I think his strength and energy came from the brandy he took every night.

Father's vegetable garden kept us well supplied during the Japanese occupation. Due to his planting, we did not suffer too much from the privations of the war. We were even able to sell at Lorong Tai Seng market any vegetables that were extra to our wants. Sweet potatoes and tapioca filled our hungry stomachs, the tapioca leaves made excellent curry soup, and the beans and the eggplants provided us with a new kind of treat every day.

We were now under Japanese rule. Singapore was renamed Syonan-to, and we became part of the Greater East Asia Co-Prosperity Sphere. The local newspaper, the *Straits Times*, was renamed the *Shonan Times* (later the *Shonan Shimbun*), and we were told to observe Tokyo time, which was two hours ahead. Owners of shortwave radios were ordered to bring their radios to police stations by a certain date for the shortwave capability to be cut off. Anyone found afterwards with a shortwave radio would be beheaded as a spy. There was much apprehension and uncertainty.

All sorts of rumours were floating around. *The British were coming back soon*—false hope. *Incoming Japanese soldiers had slaughtered a whole village of young men at Lim Chu Kang in retaliation for the stand put up by the Chinese volunteers at Batu Pahat*—this news spread like wildfire. As a warning to all, four severed heads were stuck on stakes and placed two at each end of Elgin Bridge off North Bridge Road.

I was curious. In all innocence and without a fear, I cycled to see the heads. On my way, there were many sentry checkpoints. At each one, you had to get down from your bicycle, bow to the sentry, sometimes submit to a body search, and then, hopefully, be allowed to proceed. If you were slow to bow or did not do so, you were given a slap by the sentry who shouted "*Baka!*" (Stupid!), and made to stand in the hot sun at the side of the road for long hours before being allowed to go on your way.

The severed heads were a gruesome sight. I wanted to gag although I was at a fair distance. This was the first time I had ever seen human heads without their bodies. How could humans be so cruel to each other, I thought, as if people were chickens hanging in the market.

One day, I heard there was work available for menfolk at the nearby Aik Hoe Rubber Factory on Kim Chuan Road. Together with others, I went eagerly to register. Some brought food and water along, expecting a long day of work. We all squatted in the open space on the factory grounds, waiting.

As we were called, one by one, we got up and bowed to a Japanese officer sitting on a chair. We stood mutely before him, undergoing his scrutiny. He gestured his decision to each one, either sit down on one side, or go home. Those gestured to sit down were hopeful they would be given work, while those waved home were disappointed to be rejected. When it came to my turn, I got up, made a bow before the soldier, and waited for his judgement. He pointed me to the group of people sitting down. I eagerly took my place.

Towards evening, our group was told to board a lorry. A Japanese officer passing by pointed at me and motioned for me to leave the group. I was reluctant to do so. However, he waved his hand and pointed at me again. I had to leave the group and head home. How disappointing to be rejected at this last moment, after waiting the whole day with high hopes. It must be because I am too young, and too skinny, and too small in size, I thought to myself in frustration.

I returned home, and received a good scolding and lecture from my father when he heard my story. He had been worried and was wondering where I had been all day. He said that if I wanted work, there was much to do on the estate. Neither he nor my brothers had gone to the Aik Hoe Factory.

It was only many days later that I learned that the men that had boarded the lorry never came back. Their families waited days, weeks, and months, but the men never returned. Rumour said they had been taken by lorry to be shot and killed at the Pasir Panjang beaches.

How lucky I was. If it had not been for the Japanese officer, I would have been gone. God must be taking special, good care of me. I felt very humble after that.

Time in Waiting

SINGAPORE came under Japanese military administration. Things resumed some normalcy, despite disturbing rumours of torture and interrogation by the Japanese military police (the *Kempeitai*) at the YMCA and the buildings on Oxley Rise. People went back to their homes and started work again.

The house began to empty. My two elder brothers left to return to their work and living quarters, bringing their wives with them. My eldest sister returned to Seremban. All but one of my brothers went back to work during the Japanese regime: Siew Guan to the hospital, Siew Hui to the Police, Siew Ek to the lab at the Municipal Building, and Siew Boon to Telok Ayer Chinese School. Only Siew Tee did not return to his job as a Morse code wireless transmitter at the Paya Lebar Wireless Station. He was afraid that the Japanese would arrest him, as the station had been a British military establishment.

I had finished my schooling and should have been looking for work. Now that Singapore was under Japanese occupation, though, all my studies seemed to be of little use. There was now a new language, Japanese, to learn. News came that the ship carrying the Cambridge exam papers for my year had been bombed and had sunk off the coast of India. My qualifications were lost at sea. I consoled myself with the thought that since the Japanese were now ruling Singapore, an English qualification would not be important to get a job.

As we waited for things to settle, there was nothing for me to do in the meantime. I spent idle days playing Chinese chess with the shopkeeper, Ah Chan, whose shop was on the other side of the road, down from our house. I applied myself to learning how to play the piano, starting with C on the keyboard and laboriously comparing notes in the hymnbook. I knew something about timing from my violin lessons with Bian's husband, so I struggled along, learning hymns note by note. I got better and better, and after a time, could play most of the hymns in the book. I discovered how to transpose music a semitone lower (my formula was: turn 1 sharp (G major) into 6 flats (G flat major), 2 sharps (D major) into 5 flats (D flat major), 3 sharps (A major) into 4 flats (A flat major), and so on; try it, and you will see how it works). The pastor encouraged me, saying that he hoped I would be able to play for church service one day.

One of my schoolmates, Koo Cheok Chuan, visited me, and played some tunes from the piano books left by my eldest sister, Soon Teck. I was very impressed, and I fell in love with one piece in particular, *The Maiden's Prayer*. I told myself, I must learn to play it. I practised hard the many descending octaves, arpeggios, and trills in the piece, and soon was able to play it from memory. I also learned other pieces like the *Farmer's Song* and *Fur Elise*, and was delighted with my progress. My brother Siew Ek would play jazz tunes when he came to visit, and I watched him carefully. I was soon able to play *La Paloma*, *Over the Rainbow* and many other songs in a jazz style.

Some days, I pedalled to town on the old bicycle (unwanted by the Japanese soldiers). I saw British soldiers picking weeds at the playing field (the Padang) in front of City Hall. There were still checkpoints with Japanese guards on various streets. I had to get down from the bicycle at each one and bow to the guards before being allowed to go on my way.

My sister Bian had some left some of her things at the old house and wanted them brought to her father-in-law's house at Telok Mata Ikan, Bedok, where she lived with her husband. I was asked to help. My brother-in-law, Siau Heng (the violinist), borrowed a three-wheel cycle and loaded her things on the back. We cycled all the way with Siau Heng pedalling the three-wheel cycle (sometimes getting off to push), and me helping him to tow it along with my old bicycle. It was hard, heavy work, and we passed many sentries before finally arriving, exhausted, at his father's house. We had travelled a muscle-breaking journey of over fifteen miles in the hot sun for the whole day to reach our destination.

Siau Heng's father lived in a small attap house by the sea. A Chinese doctor (a herbalist), he was a venerable old man with a room full of Chinese books. He called me over and checked my pulse, his fingers dancing on my wrist. Smiling, he gave me a Chinese prescription for herbs that, he said in his Teochew dialect,[17] would give me strength and good health. On some evenings, a sweet smell of opium pervaded the house. I wondered if the herbalist doctor was enjoying a smoke or if he was concocting some Chinese medicine for his patients

My brother-in-law used to go fishing at night for *ikan parang* (wolf herring, or *sai toh* in Hokkien), and he invited me to go out with him. I spent many days at the house, and at night, went out to sea with him. In a small sampan,[18] we slowly let out a fishing line with many baited hooks, taking care not to get it tangled. We sat patiently and waited without a word for hours, holding the line firmly all the while so as not to hook ourselves at a sudden bite. When the line jerked, we knew we had hooked a fish. We would slowly draw in the line, carefully avoiding the hooks. We were happy when we returned with some fish,

---

[17] A Chinese dialect, known in Mandarin as Chaozhouhua.
[18] A flat-bottomed Chinese wooden boat.

but sometimes, we came back hungry and downhearted with nothing. How unlucky we were. The fish must have gone away for a holiday, I thought.

It was really lonely and hard, spending the whole night without talking in a small boat rocked by the waves, vulnerable to the sky and to the elements, hoping to get some fish. It was worse when it rained. We sat cold and chilled, rainwater dripping from our hats into the boat. We had to bale out the water in the sampan too. There was lots of time for reflection while waiting for the fish to bite. Memories of my early years, recollections of schooltimes, and thoughts about what I would like to do in the future passed through my mind.

I came to realize that I was on my own now, my studies were over, and it was up to me to earn a living. The world was not as easy as it appeared to be. I had to do something to better my life.

Restless and free, I cycled all over town, hoping to find something to do. It was much safer now, and there were no checkpoints. Cycling along Upper Serangoon Road near the church one day, l came across a Japanese language school. It was open to all. No harm in learning a new language, I thought to myself; at least one would be able to understand what our new rulers were saying. I enrolled and applied myself diligently to learning the different Japanese scripts. I was soon able to manage a few words and phrases in Japanese. I studied at the school until I passed the advanced class.

Some of the neighbours heard that I was learning Japanese, and they asked me to teach their children. I rented a small house on Paya Lebar Road and started a small class for boys and girls from the Chinese school nearby. I taught them what I had learned.

A carpenter, Ah Kee, wanted to rent a room at the house, and I agreed, thinking it would be good to have a person in the house as it would otherwise be empty at night. I discovered that Ah Kee was a master of many trades. He was an ice cream seller by day, and a shoemaker and a repairer of watches, clocks, and cane furniture during his free time in the evening. I learned from him how to make delicious ice cream and how to repair cane furniture, but could not learn how to wind up the main spring of a watch. It was too delicate and difficult for me.

At that time, there was an area around Rochore Canal Road called the Robinson *petang* ("afternoon/evening" in Malay). Actually, it was a flea market, a "thieves bazaar," where you could get all sorts of things at very low prices. My eldest brother, Siew Guan, had a lot of cotton drill trousers that had been made by our tailor, Kwong Sun, on Selegie Road before the war. As my brother no longer wanted them, I sold them gradually at this flea market. I moved on to buying coats, which I stored and sold at the rented house. Old clothes fetched good prices, and there was a brisk exchange. I did not realize I had become a sort of junk dealer.

I soon tired of teaching Japanese and selling old clothes. Meanwhile, the Japanese had divided Singapore into counties (*ku*) and appointed civilian "volunteers" to help in the distribution of rations. Through a three-star system, rations of noodles and cigarettes were given out at a fixed price. Our three-star member (*kuchō*) was De Silva, who lived at Serangoon Road near the Youngberg Hospital. My father was appointed a two-star member under De Silva, and Father recommended me as a one-star because I knew both English and a little Japanese. With the help of our shopkeeper friend, Ah Chan, we distributed the rations and sold the balance. The income from the sales gave us some compensation for the work involved in collecting and distributing the goods.

But I was soon restless again. Everyone was working, and I was jobless. I took my old bicycle and cycled all over town looking for work. My second brother, Siew Hui, who was Chief Clerk at the Beach Road Police Station, recommended me for a position as a clerk at the Marine Police Station. I applied and was accepted.

My Japanese came in useful. I was handed the job of making out the monthly payroll. Writing out names in Japanese in *katakana* every month required painstaking attention. All the names of some eighty police staff had to be written without mistake or omission, as there were carbon copies underneath the original. It was good practice for my Japanese.

I was also in charge of travel permits, in which I wrote out names, addresses, and purpose of travel in Japanese. I made a chop bearing the Chinese character "林" for my family name, Lim. This character was read as *Hayashi* in Japanese. Instead of signing travel permits by hand, I stamped the documents with my chop. Everyone was eager to get the travel permits I issued, as with two chops (the chop of the Police Chief, and my own), they were seen to carry much authority.

One day, I was called to Clifford Pier by the Japanese Military Police (the *Kempeitai*). They had come across some of the travel permits I had issued. An officer questioned me and wanted to know who had stamped "*Hayashi*" on the permits. On learning that it was me, he raised his hand to slap my face. In Japanese, I quickly told him to hold on—I was the man in charge, and *Hayashi* was my name. If he did not believe me, he should phone the Japanese Police Chief at the station where I worked. He did, and after a brief exchange with the Police Chief, relented, and told me to go. The Police Chief must have said some good words on my behalf.

With my little Japanese ability, I became the interpreter in the station. The two Japanese officers, the Police Chief (*Shōchō*) and his assistant, were quite friendly to me.[19] They wanted to send me to Tokyo for further studies and training, but I declined, and as an excuse, said that my father and mother were very old and that there was no one else to take care of them. The police staff (inspectors, detectives, officers and other clerks—mostly Sikhs and Malays) were also very friendly. They gave me many privileges, perhaps because I could speak directly to their Japanese chiefs and would be able to help them if they were in trouble. Once, I rode the police motorcycle back home and nobody said a word. This was irregular as only policemen could use such vehicles.

Gambling stalls appeared all over the city, in streets and at the New World, Happy World and Great World amusement parks. The stalls were doing a roaring business and gave "bonuses" to the police in charge of their district. Merchants passing through our police checkpoint next to Cavenagh Bridge at Boat Quay would often invite the police into their shops, and give them some fish or goods that they were carrying. With their gift offerings, they hoped the police would let them through and "close one eye" if they brought in contraband at the same time.

The police sometimes gave me a share of these offerings, and who was I to refuse. I often brought home gifts of fish and food. With my job, I now had enough food, and money to spend. I bought a green Raleigh gent's bicycle with hub brakes.

The Japanese had replaced the Straits dollars in use in pre-war Singapore with their own currency. These Japanese notes had a picture of a banana tree with bananas and soon became known as banana notes. The first few notes had serial numbers, but later, notes appeared without any numbers. There were rumours that military units were printing their own notes (I think there were also counterfeiters). As inflation spread, people began carrying their banana notes in bundles. I, too, feared the banana notes would lose their value, and now and then, I exchanged my Japanese money into Straits dollars through the black market. The rates would rise and fall dramatically, depending on the rumours of a British comeback. Some people were still hoping for a return of the British.

---

[19] After the war, the assistant to the Police Chief sent me a letter care of the police station. He was operating a driving school in one of the suburbs of Tokyo, but had lost touch with his chief.

During lunch one day, I noticed people swimming in the Singapore River. The river at low tide was dirty, and sometimes there was a dank smell of mud. But at high tide, the water was clean as it came in from the sea. Usually there were *tongkang* (Chinese junk boats with sails) going up and down the river, but at high tide, the area was clear because the boats could not sail under the bridges. It was during this brief period of time that swimmers ventured into the river.

At the bend of the river near the Marine Police Station, next to Cavenagh Bridge, the Singapore River was several times wider than it was elsewhere. I thought it would be an achievement if I could swim the few hundred yards across to Boat Quay on the other side, and back. It did not seem to be that wide. I felt that I could do it.

The next day at lunch break, I put on my swimming costume and struck out for the other side. It was further than I thought, and there was an undercurrent pulling me towards the sea. However, I was determined not to give up, and managed to swim across and back. I was happy with my achievement. At least I could boast that I had swum across the Singapore River.

My sister Soon Bian and her husband came to live with us on the ground floor of the old house. Her husband, Siau Heng, had lost his lucrative pre-war chauffeur and car-rental business at Changi, as his fleet of limousines had been taken by the Japanese military. Bian had been a nurse in Muar (in Johore) and was the belle at the nurses' parties when she met Siau Heng. At home, she registered as a midwife, and in no time, she was delivering babies throughout the whole village. She rode a sturdy lady's bicycle with her midwifery bag hanging from the handle bar, and was on call day and night. She did a booming business and was paid mostly in cash but sometimes in kind. More than once, she brought home life chickens tied to her bicycle, given by households as payment for her midwifery services.

Bian was famous as a good cook, and with her in the house, we often had a feast on a Sunday, when most of my brothers and sisters came back to visit and I brought home the food ("gifts") given to the police by the merchants. My third brother, Siew Ek, often invited his friend Balu from his office, and together, we had many a treat of Bian's delicious cooking, and ice cream made by me with Balu's help. Balu, a talkative and jolly Indian, proclaimed our meals "gala" celebrations.

I had now been playing the piano for church service for almost two years, and could almost play my favourite hymns from memory. When the notes in a hymn were too high to sing comfortably, I transposed the music to a lower key, using my system of converting sharps to flats. The congregation was delighted by this trick! I also learned some simple pieces to play as introductory music. My favourite piece was still *The Maiden's Prayer*.

I was invited to play for a wedding, and I played the *Bridal Chorus* from *Lohengrin* as the bride walked in, and the *Wedding March* by Mendelssohn as the bridal pair walked out, and several other pieces in between. I managed to get by, but thought I should take up piano lessons to improve myself. I signed up with the De Souza brothers at their shop in the Adelphi Hotel Building on North Bridge Road.

But I was getting very busy, and soon had to discontinue my lessons. I also told the pastor to find another pianist for church service.

My mother wanted to visit my sister Soon Geok, who had married and was now living in Sitiawan in Perak. I was reluctant to go—trains were crowded, services were irregular, and there were often breakdowns. Also, Communist and underground fighters were active in Malaya, sabotaging trains and disrupting services now and again. I did not know how we could get there safely. Sitiawan itself was supposed to be the hotbed of the Communists. It would be a dangerous spot to visit. But my mother wanted to see Geok, and I had to accompany her or else she would go alone.

I wrote out a travel permit for Mother and myself, and had it stamped by the Marine Police Chief. I then went to the Tanjong Pagar railway station with my mother to buy our train tickets. There was a very large crowd waiting. I was desperate. There was no way we could compete to buy our tickets.

I noticed a Japanese soldier at the checkpoint, and I approached him, bowed, and showed my pass. Speaking in Japanese, I explained that I was from the Marine Police, and that my mother and I needed to travel to Perak to see my sister who was very ill—could he help us? He looked at my mother and me, and then waved us to the ticket office where we got our tickets. We were very lucky.

After a long, tiresome, and hot journey by train and then by bus, we finally arrived in Sitiawan. There, we met my brother-in-law, Keng Thian Lai. He and my sister had met while they were both studying at the Malayan Seminary. He, too, came from a large family that owned a coconut plantation. There were thirteen brothers and sisters, and he was the eldest.

We spent several days with my sister and her husband. We were treated as honoured guests and given tasty dinners, but all the time I wanted to return to Singapore. I was afraid and apprehensive, staying in an area know for Communist and resistance activities. My brother-in-law wanted to give me an outing, and he took me fishing at Lumut, some distance from Sitiawan. I didn't know we could swim in the sea and did not have my swimming trunks with me. I had to jump into the water with him without any clothes on. I had a very short swim only and did not enjoy it.

Finally, we returned home, again by bus and train. I was glad to be home. I wondered that we had been able to make such a long and difficult journey safely.

My fourth brother, Siew Tee, had not reported back to work at the Kim Chuan Road wireless station, as it was now under Japanese control. Among my brothers, Siew Tee was closest to me. He was always taking care of me and encouraging me to do noble things. Once, when as a child, I broke down in tears at school, suddenly missing my sisters who had gone away to Seremban to study, he came and took me home. He was a very loving brother to me.

Siew Tee had a heart ailment. He was normal most days, but every so often, his heart would give him trouble and he would be bedridden, unable to do anything for a few weeks until he felt better. He finished his Senior Cambridge and must have had good results as he was able to enter Raffles College. I remember him coming back from his first day at college, all smelly, dishevelled and sick. He had been ragged (I think it was the custom in those days to rag everyone on their first day in college). I suppose he had not mentioned his ailment to anyone. He was not supposed to do any heavy manual labour because of his health condition. Before taking up his job at the wireless station, he worked for a while as a teacher, in Kuching, Sarawak, and also at the school set up by his friend, Daniel E. Sundram, on Upper Serangoon Road.

Siew Tee was very sympathetic to the plight of British soldiers who were now prisoners of war. He often secretly smuggled food to their prison camps. One day, returning from another of his dangerous missions, he was stopped at a checkpoint. The Japanese soldiers forced him to work non-stop, carrying heavy loads, until he collapsed. He returned home very ill and was sick for many days. The doctor said his heart had been damaged by the work he had been forced to do. He never fully recovered, and was often laid low by his ailment. He knew he had not long to live. He confided to me that he had written a letter of farewell and showed me where he kept it, in his Bible.

One day, he became very sick. The doctor gravely noted that he had only a few hours left to live. We laid him on a bed in the circular hall at the front of the house. Miss Tan, the woman preacher, came, and all of us sat by his side, watching his laboured breathing. Suddenly, it stopped. Everything was silent. He was gone.

Miss Tan burst into tears. She had been very close to him. I remembered his letter and went to get it. We read his words in deep sorrow. Apart from a few simple instructions regarding his personal effects, his letter was full of religious inspiration and exhortation. Everyone was moved by the message he had left us. He was such an earnest Christian, always helping people and thoughtful of others. He was only twenty-six years old when he died.

My sister Bian was heartbroken and could not be comforted for many, many years.

I went to Seremban by train to see my eldest sister, Soon Teck, and was treated royally by her. Soon Teck was a nursing sister at the hospital. At home, she had a "black and white" *amah*. These *amahs*, so called because of the uniform white tunics and black trousers they wore, were known to be the best housekeepers and nannies one could find. My sister's house was spic and span, and everything was regulated like a hospital. There was a fixed time for meals, we had to wash our hands, hold the fork and spoon in a certain way, and use napkins at mealtime. I put on my best manners and was very careful. After dinner, my sister, who played the piano, would often entertain me with her many pieces of music. Or we talked of home or matters of general interest. After a week or two, not being used to such formality and neatness, I was uncomfortable and homesick, so I returned home.

The British Return

IN 1945, the city was full of rumours that Japan had suffered reverses. There was hope that the Allies would return. We didn't quite believe what we heard until some B-29s (Allied planes) flew over the city and dropped a few bombs. They were beautiful four-engine planes, and they seemed to fly around the sky without much opposition. Father's underground bomb shelter was hastily restored. We were afraid there would be bloodshed if the Allies tried to land in Singapore. We knew the Japanese soldiers would not easily give up without a fight.

Startling news came suddenly that Japan had surrendered. We heard that two very big bombs had been dropped in Japan by the Americans; many thousands of Japanese had been killed, and because of this, they had surrendered. The war was over. When the British soldiers landed, everyone was relieved and happy. It was back to the old regime for most people.

Singapore was now again under British rule. We could go about freely without fear. I spent some time wandering about the city on my bicycle. I was not keen to report to work at the Marine Police Station. I felt that with peace, I should go for further studies, or start something new. But what, I did not know. I was groping in the dark.

A New Start

D URING my school days, as I cycled to school, I was always dreaming that
I would do something different with my life. I liked the idea of becoming
a businessman and being my own boss, rather than working for the government as most of my brothers did. Looking around, though, I could not find
anything interesting. After a while, since everyone else was working and I was
not, I felt lost. I thought I should report back to work and try it temporarily. I
asked to be transferred to the Paya Lebar Police Station as it was nearer my
home.

However, after working for a month or two, I was restless. I did not like the
police work. I gave twenty-four hours' notice and walked out. I had to pay a
month's salary as default for not giving the required one month's notice, but I
did so happily. I felt as if a load had been lifted from my shoulders. I was opti-
mistic that there would be something more interesting for me to do. I went out
once more looking.

While wandering around town on my bicycle, I noticed that there were very
few taxis in the city. What taxis there were were always full and doing a roaring
business. During those early days of the British Military Administration, there
were no licensing and inspection requirements for taxis. Anyone who had a car
could use it as a taxi. I decided to buy a car for use as a taxi.

My brother-in-law, Siau Heng (Bian's husband), introduced me to a mer-
chant friend of his on Purvis Street. The merchants on Purvis Street were from
Hainan,[20] and spoke Hainanese instead of Hokkien. They did not speak much
English. Siau Heng was Teochew but could speak fluent Hokkien (our dialect)
and Hainanese. As I knew no Hainanese, I could not have done without his
introduction and his help.

His friend showed me an old, box-shaped Morris 8 Saloon. The car must
have been at least ten years old, a 1936 model. The price was $6,000, but I could

---

[20] An island in the South China Sea. The Chinese from this island speak a dialect,
Hainanese, which is a variant of the Chinese Min-nan dialect.

pay by instalments. Was this an outrageous price? I did not know anything about cars. As I wanted a car and only had a little money—not enough to pay the full amount all at once—I felt I could not bargain. Using the Straits dollars I had exchanged from banana notes during the Japanese occupation, I put down a small down payment, signed some papers, and took over the car. Bian's husband guaranteed the loan, which was to be paid in five years.

I did not know how to drive at all. The closest to driving I had got was when my brother Siew Hui sometimes allowed me to hold the steering wheel and steer as he drove the family car. I found that it was quite difficult to keep the car going straight.

Nevertheless, I was confident I could drive my newly acquired car. I got into the Morris and with eager anticipation, engaged the gears and let go of the clutch. The car jerked and bounced like a wild horse. I tried to stop, but stepped on the accelerator instead of the brakes! Luckily, there were no cars or people in front. Driving home, I had a few hair-raising, narrow escapes, but I reached home safely.

I did not have a driving license, but the police were not so strict at that time. After some practice driving, I drove to town. I had to make money to pay for my instalments. I was very nervous on my first trip. I missed people and cars by inches, but managed to get along. Soon I gained confidence and was driving like an expert. I became a taxi driver.

I decided that since I spoke English, I should concentrate on picking up British soldiers instead of civilian passengers. The soldiers were willing and able to pay higher fares. From Clifford Pier to Katong, I charged a fare of $15, and from town to Changi base, $25, or more. Soon I was driving day and night. The money came easily. I made hundreds of dollars every day. I could have made more, as the soldiers often wanted girls. But I refused to be a pimp and said I didn't know where they could be found.

After a while, I thought I should get a license. But could I pass the driving test? Cars then all had manual transmissions and were operated with a stick shift and a clutch. Most people drove old boneshakers with faulty clutches. The driving test included a parking trial on Ang Siang Hill Road, notorious for its steep incline. Here, the examiner would ask the aspiring driver to reverse into a parking spot at the side of the road. If the driver could not do so, he (or she) failed immediately. Once parked, the driver had to start the car again and drive out from the parking spot. If the car jerked or rolled backwards while the driver engaged the gears and pressed on the accelerator, he (or she) failed at this point. Most people failed their test at Ang Siang Hill.

I knew I could not pass. So I bought a driving licence. It cost me $30. What was the use of spending money to take a test that I was sure to fail when I could buy a licence? I didn't know I had bought a bogus licence until I tried to renew it when it expired after a year. As there was no record of my licence at the police station on Maxwell Road, I had to be tested for a new one. This time I passed the test easily.

With the money I made, I decided to expand and buy more cars. I bought two others, and soon had drivers leasing my cars at $40 net a day. As time went on, more and more cars came on the road, and the taxi business became less profitable. The drivers who leased the cars drove the whole day, clocking over a hundred miles, wearing out the engines, brakes, and clutches. The repairs were often very expensive. I realized that only owner-drivers could make money, as they would take the trouble to take care of their own cars. I sold the cars while they were still running to our shopkeeper friend, Ah Chan, who had been enviously watching me.

Raja Service

I then bought a motorcycle—it was much better than cycling—and went from place to place looking for something to do. At a coffee shop one day, I met Rajagopal. An Indian, he was a contractor who was also looking for business. He had experience but no transport, and I had transport but little experience. After a few coffees, he suggested we join forces. Interested to learn his business, I agreed. And so daily, I rode my motorbike with him behind on the back, going from one military base to another, looking for opportunities. A strange partnership.

We scanned the newspapers at the coffee shops but came up with nothing. Until one day, I saw an invitation to tender put out by the British Army in the *Straits Times*. The Army was looking for transportation services. The winning contractor would lease 140 lorries from the Army, maintain the lorries (purchasing petrol and spare parts from the Army), and provide transport to the Army for a year. After this period, the contractor had the option to buy the lorries at a set price. I told Rajagopal it was a good opportunity since I had relevant experience operating taxis. So together, we went to Fort Canning Military Headquarters.

We met the officer in charge, a Major. I had to present ourselves and convince him that we were qualified. I told the Major how my father was a pioneer in Singapore and even had a road named after him by the British Government. We had been hard done up by the war, and our family had lost most of our money during the Japanese occupation. I had run a fleet of taxis, and my partner had experience as a contractor. We were loyal British subjects, and if he could help us, we would be very grateful.

The officer gave us a tender form and told us to return it with a deposit as guarantee. We were very excited, but really, what chance did we have of getting such a contract? We were young and inexperienced, and all we had was hope for the future and the belief that we could do it. We did not even have the money for the deposit.

I spoke to my sister Bian and asked her whether she could lend me some money for a new business. She asked me how much I needed, and when I told her, she gave me the money without asking for details. I don't know what she saw in me to have so much confidence and faith. With the money and our signatures on the tender form, we went to the Major and again asked him for his help.

After a few days, we received news that our tender had been accepted. We had succeeded against the bids of the bus companies and several other transport companies! We were overjoyed. Perhaps the Major had seen us as young and enterprising, and wanted to give us a chance. Or perhaps we were just plain lucky.

We needed a name for the business, and my partner very cleverly suggested "Raja Service." *Raja* was the Malay word for "king." Yes, we would be the "King" of the lorry business. It was only later that I realized *Raja* was part of his name.

We soon found that we had ventured out of our depth. We had little money and very little experience in running the service for which we had contracted. First, we had to find a yard to park the lorries. We hunted all over town until we found a vacant lot near MacPherson Road. About an acre in size and fenced, it was ideal.

Next, we had to insure our lorries. How could we find an insurance company that would insure on trust? We did not have enough money to pay insurance premiums in full. Bian again came to our rescue by introducing her friend, Lo Wei, an agent for the Asia Insurance Co. Ltd. A young, pleasant man, Lo Wei had, during the war years, insured the fleet of cars owned by Bian's husband for his chauffeur/car-rental business at Changi. Yes, he agreed to write out the insurance, and we could pay by instalments. Lady Luck was smiling on us again.

The next thing we had to do was to recruit drivers to take delivery of the lorries. We advertised for drivers, and many came in response. When we had the required number of drivers, we took delivery of 140 lorries one morning, and parked them in our lot. It was a miracle that none were lost during transit. We organized a team of mechanics and created a space to store petrol in the lot. We apportioned a corner for the pump and set up a workshop next to it. This was done without a hitch.

So far, so good. But I was worried. I was only twenty-one, and felt too young and inexperienced for the daily work of the lorry business. I needed someone I could trust to manage the business. I approached my third brother, Siew Ek, who was in government service as a lab assistant. I told him that we could make a lot of money if the contract was well managed, but I could not guarantee success. He took a big risk, resigned from his job of many years, forfeiting his pension, and joined us. He was a very fortunate addition to our team.

The first few days were rough. There were some mix-ups when the drivers took the lorries out on their work orders. Imagine a hundred lorries coming in and going out all at the same time. However, we managed, and things began to run smoothly.

But after a few days, some lorries would not start. Others had flat tires. As the lorries had been fine when we had taken delivery from the military, we suspected that some drivers had removed the good batteries and tires from our lorries and replaced them with old ones. But we had no proof. We had to get new batteries and repair the tires. We tried to check the lorries as they came in, but it was impossible to check each one. We were holding up traffic, too. The matter was getting out of hand. If things went on the way they did, we would be left with lorries that were useless. What could we do? Calamity was rearing its ugly head.

One night, a fire broke out, and I was called to the lot. Some drivers came to help and drove the lorries out of the lot onto the street for safety. Unfortunately, some bad drivers came too in the confusion. Perhaps they had caused the fire to create the confusion. The next day, six lorries were missing. We searched for days, but there was no sign of them.

One of the drivers suggested a séance. The séance master told us that the lorries were hidden behind a hill, somewhere in Jurong. We searched, but did not find. We were facing another serious setback. We already had problems with the theft of batteries and tires, and now, we had lost whole lorries. Our insurance did not cover for such losses. If they continued, we would soon be ruined. We would have to close down and go bankrupt.

We were at the end of our rope. We called the drivers together and told them that that if the losses went on, we would have to close the business and they would lose their jobs. We appealed to the drivers to help us and to help themselves.

One young driver by the name of Ah Kow, who appeared to be the spokesman of the drivers, approached us and proposed a plan. He suggested that we allot each driver a lorry. The driver would be responsible for the lorry and would be allowed to drive it home. Ah Kow promised that he would see to it that the drivers took good care of their lorries. The plan sounded promising. If it worked, it would save our company. But could such a young man control so many drivers, most of whom were older and bigger than him? We had no choice but to see how he would make out.

The mysterious young man, Ah Kow, was only about five feet seven inches tall and about 150 lbs, an ordinary person, polite and smiling most of the time. When we agreed to try out his plan, he assembled all the drivers and lined them up in front of him. He announced that each driver was to be allotted a lorry for which he would be responsible. Each driver was to take care of his allotted lorry as if it were his own. He could take it home and come back the next day for his work orders.

To our surprise, there was a vast change for the better. There were no more flat tires or flat batteries. The lorries were clean and looked remarkably well kept.

Drivers were punctual and completed their work orders without complaint. Everyone went about his work busily. Raja Services was saved from ruin.

One day, an argument began between two drivers, and they started to fight in the yard. We tried to separate them but could not do so. We really did not know how to stop the fight. Suddenly, Ah Kow appeared from nowhere. He shouted at them, and almost immediately, they stopped fighting. He went up to them and slapped each one. They took their punishment without any protest. We were amazed at the young man's influence and power. The yard was quiet and peaceful again, and we were much relieved.

Soon after, Ah Kow took me aside and said he wanted to talk to me. We walked to the corner of the yard and he said, "Don't worry. Things will be o.k. If there is any trouble, just call me." Smiling, he took from his pocket and showed me a revolver. "This will take care of most things," he said. Shocked, I managed to smile back. I told him he should be careful and should keep his revolver hidden. I thought, how foolish and dangerous to have an illegal weapon on him! What kind of a man was he? Why did he carry a gun?

In any case, things were going well. Our orders went out smoothly, and all the drivers seemed to be content with the new system. The Major allotted me an army jeep with a corporal as driver. I could go anywhere with it. I should really have tried to develop more contacts with the Army then. We were in a very privileged position as a favoured transport contractor for the Army. The Major in charge trusted us as well. I was, however, too young to think of making more money, and failed to pursue the opportunity. I returned the jeep after a few days.

My partner, Rajagopal, was happily roaming about, and my brother was doing an excellent job managing the office. Our losses and worries were over.

We tendered and won a contract to lease and maintain another 100 lorries, making a total of 240 lorries under our contract with the Army. Without knowing it, we had become one of the biggest army contractors in Singapore during the British Military Administration period. Our lorries were running everywhere and we became well known. Truly, Raja Service was the "King" of the lorries.

After a while, as some lorries began to show a bit of wear and tear, we organized a workshop with another Lim family living on Kim Chuan Avenue. Together, we employed a crew of mechanics and started a call service to look after lorries that broke down on the road (something like the road service offered by automobile clubs in North America).

The Paya Lebar Methodist Church had the use of my lorries with petrol supplied free for their picnics and Christmas carolling. The banks were amazed at the money we deposited. Once, the cheque I wrote to pay the Army for leasing and supplies came to over a million dollars. I thought of the days when I was cycling to school with the cars leaving me in their exhaust. Here I was at twenty-one, signing a million dollar cheque. It was like a dream come true.

Every day, money was also flowing in. My partner wanted a car, and he bought a Morris 8 Saloon for himself. I thought I should buy one also, and I bought a new car, a Morris 10 Saloon. I paid back the loan (with interest) that I had received from my sister Bian for the business. Bian was really very generous and had trusted me so much. She was very happy to see my success.

One of my boyhood friends, Yuen Poh, one day mentioned that his mother wanted me to drop by for a visit. I wondered why. Yuen Poh's family lived in a fine two-storey house on Kim Chuan Avenue. Before the war, they had been in the gold and silver business and were known to be very rich.

I went to see her the next day. Yuen Poh's mother was a very pleasant lady. She greeted me warmly, and we had tea and small talk about my flourishing business. She mentioned that the fortunes of the family goldsmith business had declined in the war. She was thinking of selling the house and using the proceeds to send Yuen Poh to college. If I was interested, she would sell the house to me at a special price.

Of the six or seven houses on Kim Chuan Avenue, I had always admired this stately house with its large glass windows in the sitting room on the top floor. On one side across a small road was the Tan family bungalow, and in front, across a wide field in the distance, the Aik Hoe Rubber Factory. Upstairs, there was nice parquet flooring, and windows overlooking everyone and everything. There was tap water but no electricity (none of the Kim Chuan Avenue houses had electricity yet). It was really a grand house, and it was on 18,000 square feet of land.

I was interested but had no idea what to do with a house. I asked my sister Bian whether she would help look after the house if I bought it. She agreed to move into and stay in the house. So, with some help from the comprador, Lim Bock Kee, of the Hongkong and Shanghai Bank at Collyer Quay (where we had an account for Raja Services), I bought my first house for $18,000.

Now what was I to do with such a magnificent house? I was quite happy living at the old family home on Lim Teck Boo Road. At least, I thought, I could park some of my lorries in the compound if necessary. With my meagre belongings and a piano I had bought, I moved into the new house with my sister Bian.

Our lorries had military numbers on them, and so could enter military and restricted areas freely. Some drivers were making fortunes, using their lorries after work for their own businesses, buying (and later selling) goods from the military depots and transporting items into Johore. A few drivers landed in prison for smuggling. I was often asked why, with my connections to the military, I wasn't doing more to make more money.

On one hand, I wanted to listen to the drivers' schemes for making easy millions. But on the other hand, thinking of the good name and reputation of our family, I walked the strait and narrow path. The strict upbringing I had received from my parents made me take a strong stand. I could not bring myself to do anything against my conscience.

So much had taken place in such a short time. In just about a year, out of nothing, I came to have a thriving business (Raja Service) with 240 lorries, a new motor car, and the best house on Kim Chuan Avenue. And yet, nothing had really changed. I was just a youngster, little more than a grown-up boy, still with many dreams. Although I had grown a few inches after school, I was still very skinny, and I longed to be taller and to have a stronger build. A staunch Christian, I still went to church every Sunday. I had recently become the Sunday school superintendent and was teaching the pastor, Reverend Fang Chao Hsi, how to drive. It seemed that everyone was smiling at me, and the whole world was smiling too.

One day, my brother showed me an article in the newspaper, the *Straits Times*. The article related that a young man had been shot dead in the New World Amusement Park during the weekend. The young man was reputed to be the chief of a local gang (08), and he had been killed by a rival gang. I looked at the picture in the paper. It was Ah Kow! All at once, I understood his control and influence over the drivers in our yard.

In a few days, our yard was on the verge of a gang war. Rival gangs were vying for control. It was a very dangerous situation, and there seemed to be little that we could do. However, my brother Siew Ek, with the help of my second brother, Siew Hui, who was in the police, brought in a team of detectives from the Criminal Investigation Department. The head of the detectives lined up all the drivers, slapped one or two in front of all the others, and gave them a strong lecture to keep in line. Otherwise, he threatened, they would be thrown in jail. Slapping men in front of others must be an accepted way to declare one-self as the top gun, I thought; everyone, listen, or be punished and treated like a dog.

Raja Service was again saved by the skin of its teeth. The whole yard was very quiet afterwards, and business went on as usual, as before. But now, the detectives made periodic visits, and the yard was strictly under the control of the law. The drivers realised that they would be thrown in jail if they did any-thing wrong.

A clause in our contract with the British Military stated that we could buy the lorries we were leasing at the end of our contract for $150 each. Considering that the price of a new lorry was about $10,000, we thought it was indeed a good price. When Wearne Brothers, a Ford car dealer, offered to buy our lorries for $5,000 each at the end of our contract, our fortunes seemed to be guaranteed. We turned down their offer.

We were riding high. We thought that Lady Luck would be with us always, and that our good fortune would last forever. We were counting our chickens before they were hatched. But we were due for a shock.

The British Military Administration was preparing to pull out of Singapore and started to get rid of its surplus lorries. One day, the military offered for tender 300 lorries at Johore Bahru, Malaya. The tender of $3,000 per lorry was quickly accepted. Even then, prices were still strong and demand was keen. Soon, however, other lots of lorries were offered for tender—first, 300, then 500, and then 1,000. The market was glutted with lorries. Prices kept falling until lorries were being sold at $300 each. The bottom had fallen from the lorry market. How we wished now that we had accepted the Wearne Brothers offer of $5,000 per lorry! The bubble had burst, and our gold mountain had vanished into thin air.

The British Military Administration was now coming to an end, and the civil government was taking over. Pre-war regulations for commercial vehicles were being reinstituted. Taxis now needed to pass a yearly test at the Registrar of Vehicles on Middle Road before they could be plied for hire on the road. Commercial lorries also had to pass a test. Most of our lorries were not in good shape, and I feared they would not pass the test. Painting, repair of brakes, tune-up, and new tires all cost money. We would also have to get a business licence, pay commercial insurance rates and taxes—all of which we could ill afford. On top of it, we had no contracts for haulage.

I felt it was time to say goodbye to Raja Service. At the end of the army transport contract, we sold some lorries to our drivers. As we had given up the

MacPherson Road yard, we kept a few lorries on the grounds of the Lim family home on Kim Chuan Avenue (the family with whom we had organized a workshop). The rest we sold as junk, some even below our cost price of $150 each! It was a sad end to Raja Service.

Then, one day, we saw an invitation to tender for the delivery of 10,000 tons of scrap metal to the Ministry of Supply in London, England. There was so much metal lying about, in the city and in the countryside—railway tracks and bomb shrapnel lay waiting to be cleared and begging to be taken. As we still had some lorries we could use to transport the metal, we thought we should try for the bid.

We were thrilled when our tender at $28 per ton f.o.b. (free on board) was accepted. In the agreement, we had three months to collect 10,000 tons of scrap and thirty days to load the metal on the ship, after which there was a demurrage penalty of $3,000 a day for late delivery.

At first, all went smoothly. We soon abandoned the idea of organizing labour to gather the scrap and using our own lorries for transport. Buying the scrap and having it delivered was much cheaper and less trouble. We sold our remaining few lorries and concentrated on fulfilling the scrap iron tender.

We rented an office on Bonham Street, where we met and negotiated with the scrap dealers. A wily old man (an *ah pek*,[21] clad in Chinese coat and black linen trousers) came one day and claimed he knew all the scrap dealers and that he could get all the scrap metal that we needed. I went out with him several times, and he pointed out the scrap iron in different places, saying he could get them all for us. Although he did get some for us, in the end, I realized he was simply exaggerating his contacts.

Lorries carrying scrap for us were first weighed at a government station, where they were issued a certificate stating their laden weight. The lorries then delivered the scrap to our site. Here, our clerks deducted the lorries' unladen weight (inscribed on the side of the driver's cabin) from the laden weight recorded on the certificate to arrive at the tonnage they were carrying. The clerks signed for receipt of delivery of this amount of scrap. Everyday, we paid out quite a sum for scrap delivered.

At the beginning, we bought scrap metal at $3 to $5 a ton. When the scrap dealers found out about our contract, they started to corner the scrap, and prices kept rising. However, they were still within our range.

When the time came near for loading the ship, we brought the scrap metal we had collected to a designated site. According to our receipts, we should have

---

[21] Hokkien term of address for an older man.

had the required 10,000 tons, but the Ministry of Supply representative esti-mated we only had some 7,000 tons. It became clear that we had been cheated. Some lorries, on leaving the government weighing station, had dumped some scrap iron at other yards before delivering the rest to our site. Our clerks had been bribed to sign for full receipt.

We had to get another 3,000 tons to make good the full 10,000 tons of scrap. But the price of scrap was rising again. Not only that, if we were late in delivery, there was the demurrage penalty of $3,000 per day. The sky had fallen in on us. We were going to lose a lot of money. Bankruptcy stared us in our face.

In desperation, I showed the Ministry of Supply representative our receipts. I told him we had faithfully paid for and collected 10,000 tons, but had been cheated by our clerks and bogus deliveries. I appealed to him for his help, say-ing that we would go bankrupt otherwise; we had little money left. Since the scrap was for a national project, would the Ministry approach the Naval Base authorities for permission for us to cut scrap available on the base and load it directly on the steamer?

He agreed. The Naval Base authorities also agreed. We cut and loaded the mountains of broken guns, runways, and shrapnel on the base, and managed to get 10,000 tons loaded before the expiry date. The Ministry of Supply received their full tonnage of scrap iron.

But we had learned a painful lesson. I realized that business was risky and not that easy. Although saved from bankruptcy, we had lost a lot of money. There would be no revival of Raja Service.

I really did not know what to do next. My interest in business had waned, and I had lost some of my drive for it. It was a time of soul searching. Should I look for something safer—a job?

Back to Square One

I met one of my classmates, Wee Teow Kee, and he told me that our Cambridge exam results had arrived. It was five years since we had taken the exams, just at the outbreak of the war. We thought our papers had been lost off the coast of India. We had all given up hope of ever knowing how we did.

I was nervous. I was sure I had not done well in the exams, as I had not studied hard during those days of air raids and bombing. It would have been better if the papers really had been lost in the ocean. My business was gone, and I had nothing to look forward to. If I had not passed the exams, it would be the end of the world.

I did not dare go to check the results at the school for many days. But in the end, I took courage and went. I scanned the posted list from the top but did not see my name. I was getting frantic. I had forgotten the list was in alphabetical order and separated into grades. When I reached the letter "L" under Grade 1, I saw my name. What a sense of relief. Not only had I passed, but I had a Grade 1 certificate with 3 As—good enough for university. I could not believe my eyes, and it took some time before I came to myself.

On hearing the news, my eldest sister encouraged me to go for further studies and offered her financial support. She had great confidence in me and wanted me to take up medicine. But I felt I was too old, and having been in business, I no longer had the heart for study. But what else could I do? I had lost my business and did not have enough capital to start another.

For a while, it seemed as if Fate had opened another door for me by giving me my Cambridge results. As I had always been good at maths (one of my Cambridge As was in maths), I became a teacher at the Victoria Secondary School, a government school, teaching mathematics to Standard VII boys.

Teaching was unlike business. As a teacher, one gives and gives, and passes on the knowledge that one has, whereas in business, one tries to keep back knowledge and to seize advantage for oneself. I gave and passed on what knowledge I had until I felt there was nothing left.

After a few months of teaching, I joined the Teachers' Training College. However, on the first day of class, I was ashamed to find that almost all the students were much younger than me. I was like a grandfather to them. Too embarrassed to continue, I stopped attending classes. I did not think I could be a teacher anymore. I resigned from my teaching job and was again on the streets looking for something to do.

When I heard that some of my classmates were doing well with good jobs, I was depressed. I had lost the opportunity to make good in my life. Business was so uncertain, and I was almost broke. I was back to square one, and I was older too.

978-0-595-41355-3
0-595-41355-2

Harold Siew-Poh Lim,
Info: mapleleaf888@hotmail.com
Or limharold888@hotmail.com

More info and photos at :-
http://ASingaporeLifeHaroldLim.spaces.live.com/

Printed in the United States
90343LV00003B/322-369/A